One Person's Story
Following Stoma Surgery

Kate Keays

First published in 1997 and available from:
Lifeline Books
PO Box 107
BOGNOR REGIS
PO22 8YX

With the assistance of:
ConvaTec Ltd
SIMS Portex Ltd
and
Life Delta Ltd (Healthlink)

ISBN 1 84024 000 8

A CIP catalogue record for this book is available from
the British Library.

Printed and bound in Great Britain by
Biddles Ltd, Guildford and King's Lynn

A donation of £1, for every copy of this book sold, will be
divided between the support associations of UA, ia and
BCA, as listed on page 105.

Acknowledgements

I owe a huge debt of thanks to those companies that have sponsored this book. Without their help, it would never have been possible. Beyond that, it is their products that have been essential in allowing me to live such a full life.

I wish to express my gratitude to:

ConvaTec Ltd	SIMS Portex Ltd
Harrington House	HYTHE
Milton Road	Kent CT21 6JL
Ickenham	
UXBRIDGE	
Middlesex UB10 8BR	

I also wish to thank LIFE DELTA LTD (Healthlink) of 2 Windlesham Road, Shoreham by Sea, West Sussex, BN43 5AE. As distributors of stoma care products, the friendly and efficient service they provide has been invaluable. Their support of this book has enabled me to keep the cost of postage to a very minimum, thereby helping stoma patients once again.

To my parents:
In gratitude for their endless love and support

Contents

Preface

I guess that this book is something which has been growing with me for a good many years. I first became aware of the need to improve the public understanding of stoma surgery in my early teenage years. A deep desire to help and encourage others was at the centre of that longing.

In visiting those preparing for surgery, I realised that very often their greatest need was to see another person who had already undergone surgery, and was every bit as normal as the next person on the street. Beyond that, I longed to be able to reassure them that stoma surgery was not something to be feared and, for many, would give them a fullness of life that would never otherwise be theirs.

I have told my story with honesty, not because it is anything unusual, but because I long to meet that need. I hope that I can encourage anyone facing surgery to step out in confidence. I know that I have learnt lessons in life as a consequence of my own surgery and I am the richer for them.

My deepest desire is that this book should help and encourage others.

A Momentous Decision

On the 29th April 1958, my mother was taken into hospital where my imminent arrival was apparent. The birth was swift and I was taken off to the nursery, as was the custom, and my mother returned to her room.

It was not until the next day that the surgeon came to my mother and explained that there was a problem and in due course I would have to have "a small operation to close up the lump on my back." No other information was given except that I was to be taken to a hospital in Bristol where I would be seen by a specialist.

I was duly whisked off by taxi with a nurse to Bristol and later that day returned to my mother. It was at that point that my parents were told that I had a condition called spina bifida. This was caused by a defect in the spinal column allowing either the spinal cord or its surrounding membranes to protrude. My parents were told that an operation would be needed to close up the spinal lesion but that this would not be undertaken until I was about five months old.

Reference was made to my mother during that week of a spina bifida child who was doing well in an ordinary school. This, however, did nothing to quell the anxiety of my parents as the inference was that most children did not. A magazine article was also given to them but the attitudes of most only heightened and increased their fears and uncertainties for my future. When I was finally taken home, it was my parents' own tenacity that took them through the months that followed.

Life during those early days was extremely difficult for my parents. Two pieces of felt, five eighths of an inch thick and three or four inches square, had to be sewn together to make a pad of one and a quarter inches thick. A circular hole was then cut out of the centre in order that this should lie over the lump on my back. Bandages held this in place around my tummy.

However, it was a hot summer and I was soon very hot and sweaty. Two different types of cream had to be applied, one to the lump and one to the body. A further problem caused by the bandaging was that my tummy button was pushed out. A coin sewed into a hanky was used beneath the bandage to prevent this happening.

It was seldom long before the bandaging was soiled by dirty nappies and the whole procedure had to be started again. Felt was expensive and if at all possible had to be re-used, slicing off bits that were too soiled.

I had to lay permanently on one side or the other and the only time that I could be allowed to kick or move my legs was by lying across my mother's knees with the lump between.

I cannot begin to imagine the stress and difficulties that my lifestyle forced upon my family. I had two older sisters, Jane had just started school and Sal was only three years of age. Going out was both extremely difficult and hazardous, and for the most part my parents were reliant on the help of some very faithful friends.

At five months the operation was undertaken but at this point further implications of the spina bifida were brought to light. I was incontinent and it was possible that I could develop hydrocephalus at any time during childhood.

In fact the hydrocephalus never occurred but my mother, although horrified at the prospect, was always grateful that she had known the possibility. She knew that if symptoms were to occur, she would have reacted far more quickly and positively than if she had not been forewarned.

The incontinence was another matter. There was no denying that, and my parents knew ultimately that I would have to have "a bag," possibly two, if I was not to be in nappies for life. It was explained to them that the spina bifida had caused damage to the muscles controlling the bladder and this was permanent and irreversible.

In order to overcome this kind of problem, the waste products have to bypass the affected area and be removed through a man-made opening (stoma) in the body. A bag is then attached to the body to contain the products until they can be disposed of as any other person would do. I was definitely incontinent of urine and possibly of bowel. My parents had been told that any such operation would not be carried out until I was approximately nine years old but in fact a urostomy (of the bladder) was created just before my fifth birthday.

With almost no support and very little knowledge, my parents remained undaunted. They made the decision that only those who needed to know would be told about the urostomy. It was not to be common knowledge and, as far as they were able, I would be given the same opportunities as my two sisters. Jane and Sal, for their part, never saw me as any different and shared the responsibility for me in an incredibly generous way. As far as everyone was concerned, no exceptions were to be made for me. It was their desire that I should lead life in all its fullness.

Early Years Of Learning

I returned home from hospital following my urostomy operation during the extremely cold winter of 1962/3. I was very thin and it was to prove a very difficult time for my parents in many ways. The bags in those days were made of rubber with large black stoppers that screwed into the base. I regularly lost these stoppers down the toilet and it took my father's ingenuity to fix staples to the stopper and tie them to the bag with nylon cord.

The bags themselves regularly came unstuck. Not only was that a problem in itself, but the suppliers refused to send replacement bags or even plasters except after endless phone calls, pleas and explanations that they did not stay on for four or five days, even if the book said they did. Keeping an adequate supply became something of a nightmare for my parents. I was constantly in and out of hospital. Infections were numerous and many minor surgical operations were necessary.

The problems concerning my bowel were still something of an unknown quantity and constipation was an endless problem. Laxatives were a disaster and suppositories totally impossible.

In desperation my mother sought the advice of a Shaftesbury home of which she had heard and who dealt with many children of my kind. They were to provide the solution which would last for years, a product that was both gentle and effective.

It was not for many years that disposable bags were available and consequently both my tummy and the stoma were continually very sore. Infections were frequent and the stoma bled horribly.

Despite all that, my parents managed to both cope with the problems and arrange for me to start school, with my two sisters, from just a few months after my fifth birthday.

They enabled me to go to parties as any other child would, and in general terms the host very rarely knew anything of my problems. Both the headmistress and the staff of that first school were quite fantastic in taking me on with no problems or fuss whatsoever.

Jane, Sal and I with Clogs, the dog

It was approximately a year later that my father retired from the Navy and we moved to Dorking in Surrey. Different schools were considered, and in the opinion of one, I was considered not suitable as "other parents might not like it."

When I was accepted at a small private school, I was to be put in the bottom form, regardless of my previous schooling. It was not until half a term later that I was moved to the correct class and forced to catch up with what I had missed.

The only difference between myself and any of the other children was that my mother felt it necessary to take me home at lunch time to ensure that I had been to the toilet and to avoid the risk of any disaster in respect to my weak bowel. That apart, my school life was that of any other child and I am sure that that was due to the persistence and determination of my parents.

It was during those first years that the reality of school life hit me. Thankfully I had a wonderful and very special friend who showed remarkable maturity at such a young age. She was the only child who knew my secret and Kathy and I worked like a team.

As everyone knows, the "peeping-tom" craze in the toilets is an inevitable part of school life but Kathy and I had an unspoken agreement. I don't even remember how it started. I went in the end toilet and Kathy went in the next one. That way no-one could look over the top into my toilet and I was never found out by any of the children.

I did develop one other skill. In order to empty the bag, it was easiest to stand facing the toilet. However, on occasions, children did try to look under the door. I soon developed the ability to twist "facing" the toilet although my feet were still facing away from the toilet!

I suppose I have to be grateful too, for the fact that in those days, underwear was somewhat more voluminous! I never found changing for P.E. a problem so long as I was careful

The young schoolgirl!

and always remembered to nip to the toilet beforehand, avoiding unnecessary bulging of the clothes.

Kathy and I had a wonderful friendship (as did our mothers) and that has lasted the years. We spent our days together not only at school but, living a few doors apart, much of our spare time as well. Kathy and I often stayed in each other's homes and her mother very quickly became referred to as "my second-hand Mum"!

In the early days of our friendship, the appliances I had were very different to those of today. They were not disposable and at night the bag part of the appliance was unclipped from the flange stuck to the tummy and a larger one attached in its place to allow for greater capacity. Kathy's mum was very rapidly called upon to help with this as it involved stretching the opening of the bag over the flange and was much more easily performed by someone other than the patient.

We had some laughs, many failed attempts and some howls of dismay from me. But I think the ultimate was the day that my second-hand Mum prised it on with great delight only to realise that it was upside-down, pointing to the sky and unlikely to perform any function!

It was about this time that my mother had to go into hospital on several occasions and my parents were so grateful to know that I could not have been in better hands than in the care of Kathy's very special family.

I was seven years old when my parents first took us on a camping holiday. We went to Corsica with our rucksacks on our backs. I, as the youngest, had only my own things to carry but that in itself was quite a weight as I was still very small for my age. Sally and Jane each had that little bit extra to carry as well as their own things. Mum had the cooking utensils and Dad had the two tents.

They were holidays one could never forget and I stand amazed that my parents even contemplated such holidays.

Although I was by then more adept at managing the appliances, Mum and Dad had to be sure that packed amongst those rucksacks were adequate supplies of spare bags, adhesives and, probably most difficult of all, the disinfectant for the bags. If anything had run out or been lost or other problems had occurred, we would not have known where to turn for help in that country. Not only that, but trying to keep plasters stuck to my hot and sticky body in sometimes very humid conditions needed considerable patience and changing the appliance in such an unhygienic environment was no easy task.

Our first camping holiday: Jane, Dad, Sal and myself

Mum and Dad's determination to cope with any situation and never to make any exception on my behalf was something that was instilled upon my very being and it was that determination that gave me courage in later life when the need arose.

We spent our days walking and swimming and at night we would, on occasions, sleep without our tents on the beach beneath the rolling skies. We were very close to nature, sharing meal times with routine visiting rodents, listening to wild boar digging up our rubbish in the night and, on one occasion, even sharing our tent with a scorpion!

It was when I was nine years old that the disposable bags (supplied by Eschmann, now part of SIMS Portex) became available and this marked a very great turning point in my life and probably so many others too. There was one very special lady who was involved with the hospital under whose care I was at that time. She was a trained nurse with a special interest in stoma care and largely responsible for designing the new bags and getting the production line going. She fought long and hard and to her we owe a great debt of thanks. Sadly we lost contact with her in latter years and I only wish that I could today meet up and share my thanks in person for all that she did.

The problems of infections and sores were dramatically reduced by the new bags. Life in general took on a new dimension. Instead of the endless, somewhat ineffective disinfecting of the bags, now they were worn for a couple of days and disposed of.

During the years that followed we continued to camp, travelling to Corsica, Switzerland and Austria. The disposable bags made such a difference. There was so much less to carry without all the disinfectant and other accessories and the resultant improvement in my general health had made me much stronger and fitter.

It was that same year that Kathy and I also had the opportunity to go to Brownie Camp. Again I had some wonderful friends. Brown Owl was so good. She took everything in her stride and seemed to have no concern at catering for my needs.

The appliance now just needed changing every couple of days and although I was a dab-hand at doing all this, in the surroundings of a tent as opposed to a bathroom, it was a little more complicated. Kathy and I agreed with Brown Owl that we would sneak off at an appropriate moment in the evening and disappear into Brown Owl's tent. Within minutes the necessary change would be accomplished and Kathy and I would be back amongst the others without ever being missed.

By the following year when I was ten, it was agreed that I would undertake an exchange visit to a French family. For the first visit I was to go with my older sister, Sally, in readiness to undertake going on my own the following year. I vividly remember only being able to speak the present tense and not much of that either! It must have been an enormous responsibility on my sister's shoulders to know that I was, in the main, in her care.

Obviously the French family had to be informed to a certain extent of my medical background, in case of any particular problem. Quite how my parents achieved that, I never knew, but I remember the inevitable concern that the family showed for me and it was not something I liked! I hated being fussed over and did not get off to a good start.

Unfortunately for me, I arrived in France on that first visit with a dreadful cold. It was the Easter holidays and I kept a good supply of sugar coated eggs in my pocket. I rapidly called on these at the first sign of a cough. Just the remotest sign of a sneeze or a cough and they wanted to take my temperature. I certainly wasn't having that the French way!

Our bedroom on that occasion was up a set of wooden stairs with no carpet. It was the only bedroom upstairs and the toilet was downstairs. I woke in the early hours of one morning realising that I simply had to empty the bag - it was very full. As there was no way I could get down those wooden stairs without being heard and the consequent inevitable concern I would cause, I woke my sister and whispered, "What am I going to do?"

Hardly surfacing from her dreams, she replied, "Empty it out of the window." Being an obedient little sister, I did just that! It was only next morning that she queried whether she had been dreaming and discovered to her horror that I had taken her at her word!

Another opportunity which our parents generously gave us was that of riding. The riding stables were several miles away but once established, we quickly took to getting there by bike and it became a great love of my sister, Sal and myself.

It wasn't until years later that my mother suggested to me that she felt that riding had contributed to the strengthening up of my bowel muscles. It had never occurred to me at the time but I am sure that she was right. Over the years from there to teenage the muscles improved dramatically and in fact I never really had many more problems in that respect.

It was at the age of nine that my parents felt that I was able to cope with the whole school day without coming home briefly at lunch time. As a consequence of that I was able to move to another school further afield where my parents felt that I would do better.

So it was that Kathy and I parted company, at least during school time. But I was to gain another invaluable friend in Jenny. She really took over where Kathy left off and I count myself privileged to have had friends like that.

Four years later when I was thirteen, my parents saw an opportunity to buy a house in the country. It was not far from Dorking where I had spent the greater part of my life. Despite that, it was a big upheaval to leave behind all the friends in the road. We had been a very close knit neighbourhood and I knew I would miss them very much.

But I was quickly to realise the benefits of our new home. Our new neighbour had immediately offered us grazing for ponies and very quickly Sal and I both had our own ponies. My older sister, Jane, by this time was training in medicine and only living at home during the holidays.

So far as the ponies were concerned, Mum and Dad gave us our responsibilities with no exceptions. We soon learnt to keep very early hours in the morning and did all that was necessary for the ponies before going off to school. Homework and further duties with the ponies took up all our evenings and there was little time for anything else.

Within a very short time, all our holidays and weekends were filled with Pony Club events, horse shows and gymkhanas, and a new life was begun. That apart, my friendship with Kathy still remained and every so often at the weekend when the duties were done, I would cycle off to spend the day with my old friends.

The Happy Teens

Our new life held many attractions. Riding had become such a great love that to own our own ponies was something that we had never dared to dream of. But there was no denying the hard work that we had to put in.

Each morning before school we would check the ponies, feeding as necessary and ensuring that all was well. The summer months were easier but in winter the mornings were dark and cold and much of our work was by torchlight.

Breakfast now had to be earlier as the school journey was longer and there was certainly no hanging about. The evenings too were scheduled with more work and, if at all possible, exercising the ponies. By this time, we also had considerably more homework. But there was never any regret in the work that we put in, we could not have been happier.

Although Sally and I had been having riding lessons for some while, owning one's own pony was something very different. My first pony, Candy, was well aware that it didn't take much to get rid of me. One quick buck of the hind legs and I was gone every time. He used this ploy on many an occasion and I soon learnt that if you fell off, you certainly didn't let go of the reins. It could be a very long walk home if you did, and when finally you arrived bedraggled and tired, Candy would be there to greet you! I loved him for it although at times the joke wore a little thin.

My sister's first pony was a very different character. He was quite a nervous creature and very unreliable in traffic. It was always my duty to slow the cars and many was the time that we had some near misses.

It was the following year that I sold Candy and bought my second pony, Nutkin. He was so friendly and loving and every morning would call for his breakfast with real delight. I don't think I will ever forget the "whoop of delight" that greeted me when I emerged from the back door each morning.

He was so pleased to see us even if he did know food was on the way.

I think it was with Nutkin that I began to find my confidence. Nutkin had two genuine fears and those were dogs and pigs! Usually we managed to get round those problems although I always lived in terror of meeting the Pyrenean Mountain dog that lived in the village. Its size alone was just too much for Nutkin!

By this time, both Sally and I were very much involved in Pony Club activities and Pony Club Camp was on offer. Jenny was a keen and very experienced rider and she agreed to be my helper at camp. In the same way that Kathy and I had done at Brownie Camp, Jenny and I would sneak off into matron's caravan at an appropriate moment and the task of changing the appliance was soon done.

I sometimes wonder how Kathy and Jenny coped with all that I asked of them. There was no hesitation, they took me as I was and I doubt whether at the time I ever really contemplated what special friends I had.

Apart from Jenny, I had two other very special riding friends. They were Jane and Natalie. Both were blissfully unaware of my medical background. It wasn't that I didn't trust them with that knowledge. There was no need to share it. We had such fun together and they were really special times.

Jane and I always remembered with great amusement the day I fell off and was dragged down the path, banging my head on numerous boulders, before managing to stop the pony. As I in turn dragged my battered body back into action, I announced to Jane that the trees were blue and the sky was green.

Assuming at first that it was my sense of humour at work, Jane laughed till she cried. Her face dropped when she realised that I was not messing about! As things slowly started to resume their normal colour, we laughed again. That was not the case though, when a couple of days later, I went into a Spanish oral exam and there wasn't a word of Spanish to be found anywhere in my head. I stood there, totally dumbfounded, and only later was able to explain to the examiners what had happened two days earlier.

That was but one of the many occasions when I took some crashing falls. Out riding one day, one girl's pony bolted. It was literally running blind. I was in front with fences on either side and no way of escape. Two horses and their riders soon lay entangled on the ground and I felt as though I was at the bottom of the pack.

How we all escaped serious injury I will never know, but nursing an extremely painful knee and hip, the ride home seemed endless. I was miles from our house and all alone and never more grateful than then to see the comforts of home.

I stand amazed that Mum and Dad never sheltered me from any of the physical activities that they could so easily have been worried about. In fact quite the reverse, I learnt to be tough and I owe them so much for that.

During the same year that Nutkin arrived, I moved to another school. It was a good move. Although I had been happy previously, I was so much more at home in the new school. I was soon involved in the school lacrosse and tennis teams and also took part in the county cross country team trials. Sadly I didn't get a place in the cross country, which I really regretted, but lacrosse was my first love and I regularly played in the weekend matches.

Unlike my two previous schools, I knew no-one at the new school. However, I was now more confident in my own ability to handle any difficulties and did not feel the need to have the support of a friend who knew my medical circumstances. It was only later that I chose to confide in my newly made best friend.

I was still undertaking annual visits to the French family and it was during that year that I was given the opportunity to go to school in France. That was an experience that I will never forget. The first morning that I was there, they were to have French dictation. If they were struggling in their native language, I hadn't got a hope. I must have written down approximately one in every ten words and I certainly couldn't read anything back.

I did not realise it at the time, but the family's response and concern over me must have been very different by this time. I was not only accepted within the school, but was allowed to cycle the French roads, go to the cinema, go swimming, and was even allowed to stay on my own at their home while they were out. It seemed that with some people my medical history changed their whole response to me and I had to prove myself before that could change. With others, I was no different and for that I was so grateful.

Back home, it was just a couple of months later that we had a visit to the school from two members of the team of a Christian centre called Hildenborough Hall. Justyn Rees and Max Sinclair took part in several activities of the school day, in particular the morning assembly. Their talk made a great impression on both me and my best friend, Shona. Two weeks later we booked a holiday at Hildenborough Hall for the following Easter and that holiday was to mark the start of my Christian life.

As a family we had always attended church. I had been involved in the Youth Group and many other Church activities each of which had very much influenced my life. But it wasn't until I went to Hildenborough that I understood that such involvement didn't automatically make me a Christian. I had to acknowledge my individual need of forgiveness by God and personally invite Him into my life as Saviour and Friend.

It was a step that I took that Easter of 1973 and I remember so well talking to a very special member of the Hildenborough team whom we called "Grandpa". Quentin Carr's happy and smiling face is firmly etched upon my mind and I still have the letter that he wrote to me later, encouraging me in my new life as a Christian.

He wrote:

"My dear Katie,

"May I say how very glad I am that you have consecrated your life to Christ and are seeking by His grace to live for Him only...When the Lord Jesus is in control of your life, you can serve Him during every moment of every day. Your daily work, your leisure and your recreation can all bring glory to His Name...One of the commonest reasons for backsliding is the neglect of prayer and Bible study. These are to the soul what food, fresh air and exercise are to the body, so be sure to set aside some regular time each day for a Quiet Time with God...Do not fall into the error of imagining that once having presented your body as a living sacrifice to Christ that all will be well. You will find that you must give yourself afresh to Him at the beginning of each day, asking Him to fill you with His Spirit and use you to His glory."

I knew that if I was to maintain my life as a Christian, I had to make that daily commitment to God in good times and in bad and I deeply desired that I should do so. When in late 1976, I learned of Grandpa's death, I felt as though I had lost a very special friend and I am sure that many others felt that way too.

With Grandpa's encouragement to spend time reading my Bible each day, I faced life with a new direction. I made many mistakes but that new desire in my heart to know God never left me. As a teenager with all the pulls of life around me, the battles for priority in my life were strong and there were many lessons to be learnt.

Over the years I returned on several occasions to Hildenborough Hall and the challenges that their ministry brought to me were ones that deeply affected my daily living. Max and Justyn also returned to our school for another visit and soon after Gerald Coates and Eric Delve also spoke in the school Icthus fellowship. I have no idea who it was that brought such Christian teaching into the school but looking back I feel very privileged that we had it.

Just a few days after Max and Justyn's second visit, Dick Saunders came to our local town hall and he too challenged me to make my Christian life a daily commitment and relationship with God, not just a religion in name only. I guess I would have found that easier had I had the support of a lively church but living in a country village where the congregation consisted of a handful of fairly elderly residents, it was hard to find the encouragement I needed. That apart, I went to Church because I wanted to and deep within I knew that I longed to find more.

Nutkin, my pony, had one particular illness that struck him at routine intervals - colic. At times I would find him in the field in obvious distress with what amounted to extreme stomach pain. I hated seeing him like that but somehow he always made it through. But that was not to be in the summer of 1974 as I undertook my O' level exams.

I had found him in the field in obvious pain and the vet had been called. An injection was given to him in the neck but there was no relief. In fact his neck swelled up until he could hardly breathe and I spent the whole weekend revising for my exams seated in the stable beside him. Mum determined that I needed my sleep for the exams and she and Sal camped out in the garden beside Nutkin's stable.

Next morning Nutkin's distress was obvious and as I left for school I had little doubt that he should not be allowed to suffer much longer. Completing my first exam of the day, I phoned home and Mum told me that the vet had put him out of his distress. I cried buckets, I had lost a faithful friend.

Aware of my sadness and the great chunk out of my life, Mum and Dad quickly looked to find another pony and Patrick soon filled that place in my life but never the space in my heart that Nutkin had occupied.

Patrick was very different. He was a "one-man" horse. For some unknown reason, although he knew he could run away with me whenever he wanted to, he very rarely did.

Competing cross-country with Patrick

But that was not true for other people. If Patrick took exception to someone, there was absolutely nothing anyone could do about it. Never more embarrassing than the day I offered a little lad a ride down to the field. He had barely put his weight on Patrick's back when Patrick reared up and deposited him in a rosebush. He would have nothing to do

with that child. And that was the way it was with Patrick -
HE chose his riders.

Thankfully Patrick took me to his heart and there were
many times when I was almost on the floor and somehow he
put me back in the saddle. He had a big heart like Nutkin
too, and I soon learnt the new call that echoed out demanding
his breakfast each morning.

One other great benefit of the busy lives that we led around
our ponies was that we had no time to get involved in anything
untoward. We certainly had no time for boyfriends or
anything like that! So easily at that age we could have been
drawn into all kinds of wrong decisions but certainly for me,
the opportunity never availed itself until I was stronger and
more mature and for that I was very grateful. It wasn't that I
didn't have a social life. Quite the reverse, but it was always
planned outings and events, never time alone to fill in my
own way and perhaps in the wrong way.

Apart from one of my O' levels where I had failed to
complete a compulsory question, I came through very
satisfied with my results and set to work on the first year of
my A' levels.

For some while I had wanted to go into nursing and applied
to several hospitals. It was to my great delight that I was
accepted by the hospital that had cared for my medical needs
for so long. They were happy with the exam results I already
had and my place was sealed regardless of any A' levels I
might get.

It was with that in mind that I longed to leave school and
spend a year working before starting my training. I don't
know whether Mum and Dad really approved of my decision
but so it was that I left school after the first year of my A'
level course.

For some little while my parents had been contemplating
the possibility of going into farming. It was a daring

undertaking and they had waited until I and my two sisters were living independently to make that move.

As I left school, Mum and Dad sold up and moved to a small farm on the edge of Exmoor. It was a very brave move as neither of them had farming experience and they had to learn everything from scratch. The kind of determination that I had seen at work so often before, giving both me and my sisters every opportunity feasible, was now to be seen again. They set up and ran the farm very successfully for twelve or thirteen years before retiring. It was hard graft with only themselves working the farm and it was a very different and improved place that they sold on years later.

So it was that I stepped out into the world as an independent person. My parents had equipped me with all the necessary skills and abilities but now it was down to me to use them aright, fight my own battles and make all the decisions.

Independent Living

It was with great sadness that I saw Patrick loaded into the horsebox of his new owner. He had been such a faithful friend and I hated to see him go. But a new era had begun. Some friends, who both farmed and did quite a bit of competitive riding, had offered me the opportunity to earn my keep working on the farm, with the horses, and also in the house for their mother.

As I said goodbye to my parents setting off for their new farming life, I arrived at my new home with great expectation and very little idea of the real world. I had forgotten that keep didn't include many necessities of life such as toothpaste, soap, shampoo and clothes, even of the most basic kind. I learnt the hard way and hard it was too.

I enjoyed working with the horses although I was to find that though I was resilient, I lacked in pure strength. Daily I fought to manhandle full wheelbarrow loads of manure up the plank to the top of the muckheap and many was the time I failed to make it to the top. I fell first and the wheelbarrow of muck followed fast behind.

Being small, I struggled equally manfully with bales of hay for the cattle that needed to be put in hayracks above my head. They had an uncanny habit of twisting round and punching me over the left ear. The indignity of it all was not going to beat me and I rapidly found ways of overcoming all but one of them - the plank to the muckheap. There we declared a truce, sometimes I won, many times I didn't.

I will never forget the day though that I felt vindicated. One of the girls for whom I was working, picked up a load of slurry in the front loader of the tractor. Unbeknown to her the front loader was faulty and as she drove the tractor forward to deposit the slurry in a trailer, it continued to move upwards until it was right above her head. As she pressed the lever to release the slurry into the trailer, she got the full benefit. I laughed till I cried. The indignities weren't all mine and for that I was always grateful.

After six months I made the break. If there was one thing I had proved during my time at the farm, it was that I was no different because of the urostomy. For most of the time that I was there, my employers had no knowledge of my medical history. I had only felt it prudent to tell them when we set off for a major horse show some distance away. We were to be sleeping in the horsebox for the days that we were there. Obviously I had to consider that I would need some sort of facilities for changing the appliance while we were away and it was easier that they should know.

I soon managed to secure a job with an insurance company about eight miles away. Unable to find any other accommodation at short notice, it was agreed that I could continue to live at the farm but would obviously now pay for my keep. The problem of the journey to work was overcome in part by the offer of a lift with the parents of my friend, Jane. They lived about three miles away and I agreed to cycle there for eight o'clock each morning and, leaving my bike at their house, complete the journey with them.

However, it was winter, very cold, often icy and cycling those pitch black lanes was not a pleasant experience. Chilblains were soon a common problem and I had several falls on the ice.

But there was always one thing to brighten that journey. A robin was there every morning. He would appear as I cycled out of the drive and would accompany me for nearly all of the three miles. Flying on ahead, he would wait for me and never was there a day when he wasn't there. Perhaps he was my guardian angel. I certainly felt in need of one, never had darkness seemed so dark, particularly as much of the route was wooded. I celebrated the day I packed my bags and left to live with my ever faithful friends, Kathy and her family.

My second-hand Mum had heard with great horror of the journey that I was completing each morning and evening and immediately offered me a place in their home. It was an exceptionally happy six months that I spent there and, being my second-hand Mum, she made quite sure that her "daughter" towed the line. We often laugh now at the times when she declared with great feeling, "Katie Brown, don't you stamp your foot at me."

I was always grateful too, for the fact that I was in such a family environment when my first boyfriend appeared on the scene. I guess I had always wondered what the reaction of the opposite sex would be to my condition, but it was something I put to the back of my mind. I was pretty philosophical about it all and made up my mind that if they couldn't cope with it, then I could do better.

As a Christian I didn't believe in sex outside of marriage and therefore the decision to tell any boyfriend about the urostomy would be through genuine friendship or because the relationship was becoming more serious. With John, I guess I told him as part of an ongoing friendship and generally he seemed to cope very well with it. Not that he really knew what was involved but certainly he didn't head for pastures new!

Living in Kathy's home gave a great stability to life that I loved but in my heart I knew that soon I wanted to take that step of independence. So it was that I moved into a house with three other girls and I felt as if I had hit the jackpot. I had a reasonable job, a nice home, a boyfriend who cared for me, good friends around me and I wanted for nothing more.

I suppose that was part of the reason why I allowed myself to drift away from the church. It had been impossible to attend church whilst I was working on the farm. There were no days off and I certainly hadn't the gall to ask for time off to go to church. I had continued to read my Bible but with nobody to help or encourage me in my Christian life, it had been hard.

When I was living with Kathy's family, I had gone back to our old church with them but once I moved out of their home the story had been different. John was a footballer and played every Sunday and I was soon well established as a regular supporter.

Despite all that, there was always a deep desire within me to deepen my relationship with God if only I could find the people to encourage me. One church in particular, I found so hard to pass by without longing to go in for a service. Interestingly enough it was a Baptist church and it was within the Baptist fellowship that I was later to become a member.

As the months slipped by, I began to realise that I had lost my desire to nurse. Through the job that I was doing I was being drawn into accounts and other administrative work. It was then that I found out about a farm secretarial course which covered not only general secretarial work but also accounts, VAT, farm records, wages and many other things. Turning down my nursing place, I was accepted for the farm secretarial course at a college of agriculture, subject to obtaining suitable results in shorthand and typing. So it was that I spent another year working and studying at evening classes ready for my new career.

It was to be an eventful year. My relationship with John was deepening and in my immaturity I allowed myself to believe that I was ready to consider a future that would culminate in marriage. Mum and Dad in their wisdom knew that I was looking at the world with rose-tinted glasses and encouraged me to think of the commitment I was making. I wasn't listening and it was with hindsight that I realised they were right. There was a whole lifetime in front of me and it wasn't the time to make a decision that was a commitment for life.

In my heart of hearts too, I knew that it was wrong for a Christian to marry a non-Christian and John didn't share my beliefs. Not that he in any way undermined them but that wasn't enough. If as a couple we would be making decisions together for a lifetime, then we would inevitably start from very different standpoints and life was tough enough without that.

So it was that, towards the end of that year, I took one of the hardest decisions of my life and ended my relationship with John. I felt terrible and I knew that I had hurt him deeply. I tried to help him understand my decision but he wasn't listening and I didn't blame him either.

My study during the year hadn't all been plain sailing either. Half way through the course I had had an accident, crashing head first down some steps in the dark. I had taken the full force of the fall on the front of my head. Rushing off to the Casualty Department I had been duly stitched up and sent home.

As ever, never to be beaten, I made my way to work the next morning looking like something out of a horror movie. By lunchtime the boss told me the joke was over and sent me home. Taking one look at my face in the mirror, I decided that I had better go and see the doctor. The swelling was so great that the plaster covering the stitches felt like a tourniquet and my eyes were rapidly reducing to slits.

It wasn't until a week later, when I returned to Casualty to have the stitches removed, with a head throbbing mercilessly, that I let on just how painful it was. "Oh, I don't suppose there is anything to worry about but we'll give you an x-ray just to cover ourselves," quipped the doctor, applying pressure to my head that left me screaming with pain.

Somewhat incensed by his apparent disbelief of my discomfort, I marched off to X-ray. Returning a little while later, the doctor pronounced, with equal disdain, "Oh, there is a slight fracture of the skull."

The shock of the accident was inevitably to show and caused a relapse of a bout of glandular fever from which I had recently recovered. The consequence of it all was that my studies were seriously affected and when the time came to go to agricultural college I had not achieved the necessary results. Thankfully the college took it all in their stride and agreed that I should still commence the course as planned.

Becoming A Wage Earner

The year that lay ahead at college was one that I could never have envisaged. It was certainly unlike any other.

Although as students we were there to train as farm secretaries, it was considered necessary that we spend the first week finding out about, and taking part in, the practical side of farming. We were therefore involved in everything from milking the cows to castrating the piglets, injecting the sheep and learning to drive a tractor and trailer. From my own experience both on my parents' farm and at work, I had quite a bit of knowledge, but for those with none, it must have come as quite a shock.

The days were not without event. We were taught how to hold the piglets between our thighs while they were being castrated, but unfortunately for one student, she did not get the hold quite right. The piglet, quite justifiably, used the opportunity to sink his teeth into her backside and I will never know who ran the faster out of the building!

When it came to injecting the sheep, as was to be expected, they didn't always stand still to receive this indignity. The horror on one student's face as she realised she had just injected herself is firmly etched upon my mind.

For any who weren't prepared, the shock of living with a bunch of agricultural students, whose practical jokes exceeded one's wildest imagination, was very great. Birthday "treats" included being chained to the railings in the milking parlour and doused with the high pressure hose. If you had your clothes on, you were the lucky one. Sometimes, I felt, the jokes were all too extreme, but I was fortunate to have one really good friend who, in all honesty, kept me sane.

Kevin was not without his practical jokes but they were all good fun and not verging on being downright dangerous as some of the others had been. I soon learnt to check my bed before sitting on it, as although the legs might be in the right place, they were not always attached.

Kevin did a good line in unscrewing parts of the furniture and leaving them to all intents and purposes in their rightful place but it only took one small movement for things to come crashing down around you and I soon developed a very suspicious mind.

I don't know how I would have survived that year without Kevin's friendship and help and yet again I counted myself privileged to have good friends like that. With so many very physical practical jokes going on around me, I genuinely was afraid that someone would do something to me which was dangerous to my person. Somehow Kevin's friendship was the "protection" that I needed. I don't think he realised that and perhaps I should have told him.

The year passed quickly and all too soon the exams were upon us. I came away very satisfied with my results and in a very short time had taken up a position as a travelling farm secretary in Devon.

Initially I had been kindly taken in by a lady with whom my sister had boarded whilst at college and she was so very kind to me. But the old hankering for independence was back and I soon found myself a bedsit with a kitchen and bathroom shared with a couple of other girls. I felt very mean upping and leaving my landlady so soon after my arrival but I think she understood.

For nearly a couple of years the bedsit became my home. It was the first weekend that I was there that it snowed and I was unable to go home as planned. One of the other girls offered me the use of her television over the weekend and that was to be the start of yet another very special friendship - with Helen.

Helen and I were very alike in many ways and we soon discovered many common interests. We quickly got to know each other's families and it was great to have found a friend so soon.

My Christian life had continued to suffer during my college days as I had never really found a local church to attend and feel a part of. I had, as before, continued to read my Bible but I lacked the fellowship and encouragement that I needed so much. So it was that when I arrived in Exeter and quickly found myself a part of the church close by, I revelled in the new opportunities available to me.

Helen and I quickly became a part of both a discussion group and a prayer group and we made some very special friends. One of those that we met was Fred. He was about seventy-five years of age when we met him and he was such a caring man. A keen gardener with an allotment, we were regularly the recipients of huge bunches of beautiful chrysanthemums that he had grown. If ever we met as a group at his house, he laid on the most incredible spread of food. He just loved to entertain and be with people.

Not only that, but we were soon a part of his regular prayer list, and along with so many others, he prayed for both of us every day and continued to do so long after Helen and I had both left Exeter and gone to new jobs. When we heard that he had died, after a long battle with cancer, just before his ninetieth birthday, we felt a great loss. He had been a very special friend.

Even as I began to be a part of a fellowship again, I felt a great desire to learn more and make my faith something that had a daily impact on my life. And so it was that one weekend I was invited to attend a charismatic church in the town.

"Do you want to be baptised in the Holy Spirit?" the preacher asked. "Yes I do," I thought, if that is what enables me to bring real meaning to my faith. Laying hands on me, they prayed for me and I felt a great sense of peace and happiness that was so special.

I came home with a very special peace in my heart and I knew that it was the start of a new beginning. I found a new understanding reading my Bible and an ability to pray in a new way. I really enjoyed the new songs that were sung within the church, although as a quieter person I did not feel able to express myself with hands raised and feet dancing.

It was during that year that I went for one of my routine check-ups. I was under the care of a wonderful man, Professor Mitchell, who had been responsible for my original urostomy operation. He was a really special person and it was a very sad day when I parted company with his great expertise, wisdom and kindness.

But on this occasion I was to have a check by an orthopaedic consultant who was to look at my back, legs and feet in particular. My feet had been giving me a certain amount of discomfort and it was for that reason that an appointment had been made.

Having checked me over quite carefully, the consultant asked permission for a couple of students to have a look at me. This was quite a common occurrence and I readily agreed. He left, telling me that when the students had had a chat with me, he would be back. Three students duly appeared, all of whom were really friendly and kind. Having asked many questions, they too disappeared, assuring me that they would return soon.

Sure enough they did return along with the consultant and about a dozen other students. The little room was crowded with onlookers, the vast majority of whom were male. It was at that point that I, dressed only in my underwear which would have been less brief had I known the circumstances, was required to touch my toes, bend at the hips and perform just about every other weird and wonderful contortion that the consultant could concoct.

As if that wasn't enough, he then asked each student in turn, "Now, what would you do to correct this problem?"

Having had just about every part of my anatomy ripped apart, re-hashed and generally re-assembled, I was feeling pretty indignant by the time I left. Thankfully I had a tough constitution. Had that not been the case, all their answers would have been enough to ensure that I would never ever have set foot in a hospital again. Never before had I had that sort of treatment from students and I counted that consultant as a very thoughtless person.

I was much enjoying the job that I was doing. Three out of five days of the week were spent at one farm where I was very quickly made to feel at home. The good friends that I made were very special and I appreciated them so much. The rest of my time involved travelling to different farms around the area and it was there that I missed the company of other people. Generally speaking, the farmers themselves were out at work and much of the day I spent alone.

Nearly two years on, I replied to an advertisement in a Christian magazine for an accounts clerk for a missionary society in London. Just a couple of weeks later, the secretary of the Mission called to interview me at my bedsit, whilst in the area on deputation work. The day after his visit I was to go home to spend a week's holiday helping with the lambing on the farm. I desperately wanted the job and spent all week longing to get back to see if there was a letter.

The job was mine and I was thrilled, but reality soon sunk in that I had to find a place to live in London. Time was short and as the days passed by I began to panic. Expressing my need of accommodation at the prayer group one evening, the curate spoke of a possible place in a Residential Hall in the East End. Within two days, I had been to London, seen and accepted a room in the Hall.

I felt sure that God wanted me within that job and when the accommodation was found I should have known that I could trust Him to help me in my new life ahead but the culture shock of arriving from the wilds of Devon to the streets of the East End was just one step too far.

My sister, Sally, drove me up to London. Somehow we negotiated our way through the centre of the capital and arrived at my new home. It was a Sunday and the dark and dingy entrance to the carpark at the back of the Hall seemed stark and eerie. Chip papers rustled in the wind in the deserted alleyway and Sal looked at me in dismay. "You can't live here," she said. I really wanted to agree with her but there was no turning back, it was too late for that. As she drove away later that evening, I felt so alone.

In fact the place was no different from any other city but I had become a country girl and the contrast was awesome. Being right on the edge of the city, that part was deserted at the weekend. It was a Bank Holiday weekend and the empty streets freaked me.

The following morning I decided to encourage myself by going shopping in central London. Setting off for the underground, I purchased my ticket to Oxford Circus. Making my way to the platform, I settled down with a few others to wait for the train. As the first one came in and the doors opened, out fell a hoard of noisy football supporters, shouting their odds. To my dismay I realised that as this train was not the one I needed, I had to share the platform with these people until the next one came along.

All of a sudden, all-consuming panic took hold. Taking the stairs two at a time, I told the dismayed ticket collector I had forgotten something and had to return home. Running full pelt down the street, I arrived in my room in the hall shaking like a leaf.

Sinking onto the bed, tears began to flow and I picked up my Bible. As the pages fell open, I read: "He tends his flock like a shepherd: He gathers the lambs in his arms and carries them close to his heart; he gently leads those that have young." (Isaiah 40:11) Those words hit home like a bullet and I knew that I had to learn to trust God to help me in the days ahead.

Those words were duly etched upon my mind in the days that followed but I always remembered them without the last phrase speaking about gently leading those who have young. It wasn't until some years later that those last words were to have the same impact as the rest of the verse.

I didn't find the adjustment easy and God was very patient with me. I will never forget one Sunday evening as I set out to walk to a very lively church on the edge of the city. The streets were as usual deserted and I felt really vulnerable. Trying to keep things in perspective, I walked on. But a noise behind me finally set off all the alarm bells in my mind and I ran, as never before, all the way to the church.

Arriving with the look of an exhausted marathon runner, I slowed to a walk as I approached the path to the front entrance. One thought, and one thought only, filled my mind. How was I going to walk home again on my own? Reaching the door of the church, I prayed, "Lord, please, help me to find someone to walk home with."

It was an enormous church filled with students from all over London. They came in groups and not having been at the church for very long, there was only one person with whom I had made much contact. The chances of finding him amongst all the people was pretty remote. Entering the building, Ian was the first person that I met.

Like some demented individual, I tore up to him and said "Please, Ian, will you walk home with me later?" Somewhat surprised but asking no questions, he agreed, and I prayed that I would be able to find him again after the service.

True to his word, Ian did walk home with me that evening. Ambling through the deserted back streets together, I asked him more about himself. He told me he was an ex-armed robber who had served time. I guess God had the last laugh!

There were other times too when the London life caught me on the hop. Fighting the crowds one day on the underground, I found myself rammed up against a rather large and hot male species as the doors closed firmly behind me.

As the crowds fell out at the next station where the platform was on the opposite side, I gratefully started to make my way forward only to find that my skirt was firmly trapped in the doors behind me. Short of taking my skirt off, there was no option but to stay where I was and pray that at the next station the platform would be back on the other side!

Determined not to make a fool of myself, I leaned casually against the doors, making myself out to be resting contentedly until the doors flew open at the next station and I was thrown out with gay abandon.

I loved the work at the Mission and got on very well with the other staff. Alan, the secretary, became a great friend. He taught me so much and as a family man with his own growing children, his advice and help was a real bonus. It didn't take him long to pick up the signs that I seemed to be making regular trips to the coast each weekend and he had a pretty shrewd suspicion that there was a man in my life! He was right of course!

Tying The Knot

It had been one sunny day in July that I had been persuaded to accompany a friend for a day out in Bognor Regis. I hadn't been particularly keen to go but had eventually agreed. I found out that my friend had arranged for us to visit several people during the day, one of whom was the late, much acclaimed writer, Rosemary Sutcliff. She was a lovely lady and I am privileged to have met her.

Later that day we went to visit one of the residents at a Shaftesbury Society home for disabled men. No contact had been made in advance and on our arrival, we discovered that it was Carnival Day. All the residents except for one were taking part on one of the floats in the procession. The only resident at the house was Mitch.

Mitch showed us around and used his persuasive powers to encourage me to buy one of the cane-edged trays that he and his friend had made. I enjoyed his company and later that week wrote him a letter to thank him for showing us around and for the tray that I had bought. He replied to my letter and the friendship began.

So it was that, just a couple of weeks later, I booked myself a room in a Christian Hotel that I had seen advertised in Bognor and set out for a weekend by the sea. I hadn't told Mitch that I was coming and he was duly surprised at my arrival on the Saturday morning.

That was to be the start of many, many trips to Bognor and I soon found a good selection of Bed and Breakfast rooms to call upon. Sometimes I was able to stay in the guest room at the home and for that I was always very grateful. Our friendship blossomed from those beginnings.

I guess the fact that Mitch was disabled and in a wheelchair gave me an affinity with him, not in any patronising way, but in real terms. It could so easily have been the other way round and I had no difficulty in sharing with him my own medical history which he knew from very early days.

By this time, I had moved from the Residential Hall and taken a room in a house with a young family. Although we lived fairly separate lives, again I was to find myself amongst people with whom great friendships were made and that was very special. I felt more at ease living a little outside London and was able to have my own car. I didn't use it during the week but I had the use of the garage and the car was there ready for me every weekend on my trips to Bognor.

Each weekend that I was down, Mitch and I went to the local Baptist Church and soon made many friends there too. It was during those early months that Mitch came to share my Christian faith.

Although to the average person there were all kinds of problems to our relationship, not least that there was nearly twenty years difference in our ages, as well as Mitch's disability, to me the last barrier had been broken.

That Christmas I spent at the Shaftesbury home with Mitch. It was the first Christmas I had ever spent away from home and I guess that spoke volumes to my family. Bognor was rapidly becoming a place that I had come to love and Mitch's friends were now my friends too. Two of those friends, Ronnie and Margaret, had been so good to us and time and again we counted ourselves privileged to have friends like that.

It didn't come as any surprise to the family therefore when I took a temporary job in the laundry at the home, waiting for a post that I hoped to be offered in a bank in nearby Chichester.

I don't think Mitch ever proposed to me in so many words. I think we just knew we were meant for each other and in March nearly two years after we first met, we got engaged.

We didn't know what people's reaction would be but the vast majority were thrilled. The family were fantastic and if they had any reservations they were certainly good enough to keep them to themselves. That wasn't always the case with others but that was something we were going to have to learn to live with.

Setting off to work with an engagement ring on my finger, I wondered how long it would be before somebody noticed. Suddenly the shout rang out, "Hey Kate, what's that ring on your finger!" "Who is he?" "How old is he?" "What's his job?" As I did my best to answer their questions, I could see them visibly deflating and very soon the conversation was over. I had pricked their bubble of the ideal romance and they didn't understand.

Our engagement party

Mitch and I had planned to get married at the end of September and all the preparations were well underway. Our biggest problem however, was one of accommodation.

Rented accommodation was quickly snapped up and rarely suitable anyway. I had only recently started work in the bank and taking out a sufficient mortgage was out of the question. I think we both began to wonder whether we would ever find a suitable place in time.

Even if I had seen God answer so many of my prayers in His own perfect way and timing, this one seemed just so impossible. And yet in His own perfect plan, God provided a flat that really was remarkably suitable and adaptable for Mitch's purposes. It did come with an extremely difficult landlord whom even the solicitor took exception to but I knew that God was in control.

We just had time to collect together all the necessary furniture, much of which came through family, and our home was made. By the time our wedding day came on the 25th September I had already moved into the flat and Mitch was looking forward to joining me.

Two hundred friends and relatives joined us to make that day really special. The Shaftesbury Society laid on a wonderful reception to complete a day that we would never forget.

Leaving the church as man and wife!

Mum and Dad at the reception

As we set off on our honeymoon, I don't think the reality of it all had sunk in. It was the start of a life together in which there would be much to learn, happy times and sad times, good times and hard times, but most important of all, a life in which God would go with us and help us, if we allowed Him.

Reading the local papers on our return, I suppose I should have been more prepared for people's attitudes to us as a couple. Writing about our marriage, we had apparently had "a fairytale romance!" Personally I couldn't remember Mitch hacking a path through the forest to rescue me and bringing me back to his palace to be married . . . but then perhaps, I just missed that bit!

We soon settled down to the routine of life. Hours at the bank were long as we were often expected to work overtime. I found meals that could be prepared in advance and were suitable for Mitch to switch on at the appropriate moment. We soon had a good routine too for the things that I had to leave prepared for Mitch. But the long hours began to take their toll, evenings and weekends were so short and I really felt that I needed to do something about it.

In the course of conversation I discovered that another small branch of the bank was looking for a new cashier. Expressing a desire to be considered for the post I felt that perhaps this was the help that God was going to provide. Although it was still a full-time job, being a small branch, overtime was extremely rare and I knew that it would give me those few precious extra hours at home.

The transfer was made and although the job included typing which was not one of my fortes, I much appreciated the benefits that it gave me. It wasn't the happiest year of my life but it was one of God's special stepping stones to other things that lay ahead. Although I continued to feel that I should reduce my hours, I could see no way of doing it. Eventually, I handed in my notice.

It seemed a pretty drastic thing to do but I had felt for some while that God was asking me to trust Him. As Psalm 55:23 said, "But as for me, I trust you." Almost instantly my resignation letter was returned to me as unaccepted and in a short time I was offered a post in Bognor itself for three days a week. We were thrilled - yet again God had been proved utterly faithful.

As we settled into the new routine, I knew that there was another great desire on my mind. I wanted to start a family. Mitch and I had talked about it from time to time but deep within I knew Mitch was concerned for my health. At the time I knew of no-one with a urostomy who had had a child and the inevitable questions lay unanswered. It was not only the urostomy itself but the fact that spina bifida was hereditary, and although I didn't know the statistics, the risk of having a spina bifida child was a very real one.

When, just a few months later, my pregnancy was confirmed, we were absolutely overjoyed but we knew too that we were setting out on a journey where the difficulties and problems were totally unknown. We would have to face each one in turn but in the certain knowledge that God would go with us.

Looking back over the years, I was so thankful for all that I had been able to do. My parents had given me every possible opportunity they could and had never sheltered me. Because I was no different to them, I counted myself no different to anyone else. In fact, I guarded fiercely that privilege of being "normal".

I don't think any of my employers had ever known my medical history. In none of their application form questions had I ever felt it necessary to say anything. The only question which would have been debatable was, "Do you have a disability?" Since the urostomy had not stopped me doing anything that I had wanted to, my answer was "No," and there it remained. I sincerely hoped that I would be able to say that of pregnancy too.

A Touch Of Pregnancy

I think the news of my pregnancy temporarily stunned the family into silence.

"We've got some special news!" I told my sister.

"Yes?"

"Well, what do you reckon?" I teased.

"You're not!" she stuttered.

Having overcome their initial shock, the family were thrilled. If they had any reservations, yet again they were good enough to keep them to themselves.

The first few months seemed much like any other pregnancy I had heard about. I felt sick from time to time but generally kept pretty well. It was only at about three to four months when my body started to change shape that I began to have problems with the particular appliance I was using.

After a word with my G.P., I was put in touch with a stoma care nurse in the local hospital. Not having had any problems previously, I was unaware that her help was available.

I got on really well with Gwen. She was ever so kind and not only helped me to find an appliance that could cope better with my changing shape but also gave me the address of another person with a urostomy who had recently had a baby.

Feeling much encouraged and wearing the new appliance, I returned home convinced that problem number one was solved. I wrote to Fiona who had had the baby and eagerly awaited her reply.

Two days later I went to make the routine change of the bag and found to my dismay that I couldn't remove the adhesive from my skin. It might just as well have been stuck with superglue. After an hour of tugging and pulling, soaking in water, smothering with adhesive remover, I was desperate.

All I had succeeded in doing was pulling part of it from the skin, making it absolutely imperative that the rest came off.

At a complete loss, I phoned my mother, dragging her out of bed, begging her to think of anything from her past experience that might help. She couldn't think of anything that I hadn't already tried.

It took me two and half hours of soaking in the bath and picking piece by tiny piece from my skin before I finally removed the appliance. The bath was full of tiny bits of plaster. I was very sore and very tired and I spent the next two weeks picking minute pieces of plaster out of the hairs of my legs!

Describing my experiences to Gwen on the phone next day we had a good laugh and I felt better. I was to learn that the hormonal changes in my body affected my skin and that in turn had caused this reaction with the plaster. Thankfully with the use of a special wipe, a thin film could be applied to the skin stopping any further problems in this respect.

In due course I was called for the routine scan and longed to be able to see the new little life that I was carrying. I discovered that there was definitely one advantage to having a urostomy. All the other ladies were required to drink as much as possible thus causing the bladder to fill up and move aside for the best possible picture of the baby.

Whilst they sat there with agonised expressions on their faces, hoping upon hope that they wouldn't have to wait much longer, for me, there was no such problem. I had no bladder, there was nothing to fill! Whilst it took a bit of persuading to convince the nurses that there really was no point in filling me up with fluid, they did eventually believe me!

There was one great fear in my mind. I was well aware that my sister, Sal, had been very much pressured to have an amniocentesis because of my history of spina bifida. She had refused to have it and I knew that I too might be under the same pressure.

I needn't have worried because, although it was offered to me, there was no pressure. Mitch and I were adamant that the pregnancy was a risk that we took and there was no question of having a termination. It was pointless therefore to undertake the test which had a risk in itself of causing a miscarriage.

Throughout the pregnancy I had been encouraged to stay on a low dose of a safe antibiotic to prevent the higher risk of urinary infection during pregnancy. I had had my doubts about this decision but was grateful that I was having no problems in that respect.

As the months rolled on and the kicks got harder and nearer to the stoma, I began to brace myself for the day when I felt inevitably there must be a direct hit, but it never came.

The pressure on the stoma itself, however, was at times excruciating and I really began to wonder how much more it could take. Despite all of that, I had kept remarkably fit and cycled to work until, at six months, I began to feel just too fat altogether!

If the pregnancy had been relatively uneventful, other things certainly hadn't. As soon as I had been confirmed pregnant, we knew that another battle lay ahead. Written into the lease of our flat was a clause stating, "No children allowed."

Even before the pregnancy, we had made enquiries into the possibility of a council or housing association property and had been told that when the need arose, they would help us. In fact it had been very difficult and, as so many times before, we had had to believe that God knew our need and would answer our prayer.

When an offer of a disabled bungalow came in the post one day, we were euphoric. Later that day we set out to view it and were utterly dismayed at what we found. The whole layout of the bungalow was entirely unsuitable and even the entrance had a ramp with no flat surface at all for someone in a wheelchair to stop and unlock the door. Feeling really confused and concerned, we turned it down.

Some weeks later another offer arrived. Not raising our hopes too high this time, we set out to view it. It was a groundfloor flat and, to our dismay again, had an enormous step as well as a very heavy firedoor at the entrance. Both had to be negotiated at the same time and even in a non-pregnant state, there was no way that I could have helped Mitch over such an enormous step holding a heavy firedoor at the same time.

Inside there were also numerous problems and had we accepted it, we would have been committing Mitch to being a prisoner in his own home. With only a couple of months until the baby was due, we were hurt and confused.

It was with great relief that just three or four weeks later we went to view another flat and were able to accept it wholeheartedly. Just a few hours later that day I was taken into hospital and declared to be in labour.

As I counted off the first hours of labour, I encouraged myself that with each hour that passed, I was one closer to enjoying the gift of new life within me. I didn't find it funny when a few hours later, the labour pains died away and it was declared a false alarm.

A day later I was allowed to go home and told that I was to rest and do nothing strenuous. Mitch and I spent a very quiet Christmas on our own and just into the new year, I set off to hospital for a second attempt.

Nobody knew with the operations that I had had, whether I would be able to undertake a normal birth. Hours on and very tired, the option was given to me, "It could be another seventeen hours or more, would you like to call it a day and have a Caesarean section?" I had little doubt in my mind that it was the right thing to do.

So it was that at twenty to two, in the early hours of the morning of the 12th January 1985, God gave Mitch and me the very special gift of a little girl, Michelle. The picture of Mitch holding his daughter for the first time was one that said it all - he was such a proud Dad.

Facing Facts

It should have been such a happy time. It was barely two weeks since the birth of Michelle and that miracle of life was there before me. But tiredness was overwhelming and Mitch was in bed with a cold such as he had never known before.

I knew that Michelle would cry any minute for another feed and I suddenly felt incapable of providing for her needs. All-consuming panic took hold of me. I honestly did not know whether, if I picked up Michelle, I might drop her or if I was even capable of changing a nappy.

After a brief attempt of explanation to Mitch, I picked up the phone and rang the number of some faithful friends, Alf and Betty. I only said four words, "Please can you come." Sensing the urgency, they were in the car in minutes but it seemed like hours to me. I paced the floor for fear that I would collapse. Purposely I paced the areas which were not on Mitch's route to the door. I was terrified that I would collapse and his route would be blocked.

Our friends arrived and weighed up my state with but a look. In next to no time Betty had set up a bed in our sitting room with Michelle alongside. I was in bed with a promise that I would only be disturbed for as long as it took to actually provide the breastfeeds necessary. The rest would be taken care of.

Sleep was a soothing balm but those black clouds of darkness were not dispersed. They had been looming large before Michelle's birth but I had not recognised them or identified them for what they were. I still didn't but at that point of crisis I was challenged to consider my emotional state.

I had always been a very independent person. It was something that my parents had instilled in me from early childhood and I was grateful for it. It had made me an optimistic person who was rarely overwhelmed by circumstances.

I could not understand anyone who suffered from depression or despair and I certainly had no respect for them. In my opinion Christians did not suffer from depression and I went so far as to doubt the validity of their commitment if they did.

What was going on within me during the year leading up to Michelle's birth bothered me, but when parental pressures brought out all that was latent within me, I felt condemned.

The weeks that followed were some of the most challenging of my life. When Michelle was just six weeks old, we moved to the new flat. Packing up all our things so soon after a Caesarean birth was something I will never forget.

The inevitable broken nights with a hungry baby were gruelling and the landlord of the flat we were vacating required that it be decorated throughout. If not we would forfeit the five hundred pound deposit that he held. This had absolutely nothing to do with the state of the flat. It was a requirement that he enforced rigidly on all tenants.

At 7.30 am the removal men arrived and we were underway. The days that followed were sheer grit determination. All of our precious friends took on a role, one friend Alf spending hours in the old flat, decorating madly.

About a week later the flat was inspected by the overseer for the landlord and declared satisfactory. As he left the building, a cheer went up by all present and never was a more heavy load lifted from our shoulders. At last we felt we could get down to the business of enjoying our new family life.

But I don't think any new mother is truly prepared for the responsibilities of a new baby. Here was a little life who was utterly dependent on me for her every need and the responsibility felt enormous in the new role that it was.

The tiredness and all that had gone before added to my load and somehow, somewhere, I needed to unburden my heart. I had kept in touch with Alan in London. I had always respected his wisdom and it was in a letter to him that I must have in some way shown the depth of my feelings.

He phoned me immediately and shared the thought that perhaps I was suffering from post-natal depression. He encouraged me that although I found it hard to read my Bible that I should try to read just a small amount each day.

As I began to look back over the past couple of years, I realised that it had been a time of enormous change in my life and whilst family and friends and those who really knew us had been fantastic, others understood so little.

Mitch and I had hit it off from the start. There was no difference between us as far as I was concerned. That obviously wasn't what the little old lady thought though when she stopped Mitch and me in the street and quite candidly asked Mitch, "Is this your wife or your daughter?" I was too dumbstruck to notice Mitch's answer.

But all that didn't change the fact that I had been brought up in a world where hero meets heroine and carries her off into the sunset. In that idyllic world, each perform their given roles and, over and above all that, the man is there to protect, help and guard. The first time that illusion was shattered was out on a drive in the country.

For some while there had been a knocking noise that bothered me but I was too engrossed in a romantic drive to put my mind to such practical matters. Finally I felt it was time to investigate and pulled into a lay-by.

Convinced that it had something to do with the wheel, I pulled furiously at the wheelhub. That was when the first nail broke followed shortly by the loss of the skin on my knuckles. Bracing myself for a further attempt, I knelt in a puddle, broke another nail, groaned loudly and fell over backwards as I lost my grip.

At that precise moment, Mitch put his head out the window and said, "What's the matter?" It was a good thing the wheelhub hadn't come off because there was no telling what I might have done with it. The romantic drive in the countryside was well and truly shattered.

The fact remained that although I saw us as no different, I was going to have to learn to cope with the reversal of many of the roles that had been laid down in my mind. Just because I loved Mitch didn't automatically change the ideals that had been instilled in my thinking.

Neither had it anything to do with the fact that I wasn't prepared to take on those other jobs. I was, but I still had to learn to do them and the hardest of all were the physical ones. The strange thing was that it wasn't managing the physical jobs that was the hardest part, it was having to do them.

Over the months and years that had followed, many such situations had occurred in one form or another. Moving heavy furniture (especially six weeks after a Caesarean section), clearing blocked drains with a baby crying for attention in the background and trying to pack wheelchairs, prams and heavy luggage into the car did absolutely nothing for my sense of humour.

It wasn't that I couldn't do the jobs, it was learning to cope with the sheer volume of work and with jobs that my mind had been brainwashed into thinking weren't mine. But with a stubborn streak and an independent nature I wasn't going to be beaten.

Alongside that, there was a world out there that understood so little about disability, and one of the biggest shocks I had when I married Mitch was that I became "disabled" too.

Sometimes it was the sheer pomposity of those who thought that the disabled were incapable of running their lives aright and other times it was the ignorance of our normalness that got me down. "Do you see each other every day?" was a question that was asked more than once. The first time it was asked I was lost for words, the second time, I had a very nasty desire to be crude.

The pomposity of those who thought we were incapable of running our lives for ourselves hit home like a knife because I felt, in a sense, that I had already had to prove myself so far as the urostomy was concerned. I had already proved that I was no different because of it and now I was being asked to prove it again in respect to my marriage to Mitch.

The ignorance was almost as bad because it meant that only those who really bothered to know us were able to make friends with us. To the rest we were to be avoided. They didn't know how to handle us and I missed their friendships desperately.

We were just so grateful for those who did accept us for who we were and as no different to anyone else. Their friendships meant the world and we honestly would never have survived without them. They helped us in so many ways and each one was special and that need for their friendship was no different to anyone else.

As Grace Sheppard said in her book, "An Aspect of Fear", "...I continued to learn the lessons of interdependence, and of the need to recognise that we all belong to one another. I became convinced that we're put on this earth not just to battle alone, or even to dole out our favours to others without expecting to receive something in return. Learning to receive became as important as learning to give without counting the cost."

We each needed each other and disability shouldn't change those values. At the heart of it all though, I knew that both those attitudes were caused in the main by genuine ignorance and I myself had been guilty of them both in the past.

Wrapping all this up with the overall pressures that we had been under, I realised that it wasn't surprising that I was struggling. I had read a comment about post-natal depression, that considering the stresses and strains of pregnancy, labour and birth, it was surprising that it wasn't more common:

"The anxieties of pregnancy, fears of the unknown, perhaps lack of sleep, concern as to whether the baby will be normal, whether the delivery will be easy, and then, when delivery has been completed, the progress of the baby (more especially the anxiety which may arise over breast-feeding), could impose an intolerable burden on any woman."

All of those concerns and difficulties had been ours together with many others.

Sadly, as happens so often, the stresses and strains of life are taken out on those closest at hand and in this case it was Mitch. I don't suppose he really knew why he had such a grotty wife but thankfully he put up with it. It must have been quite a relief to him when I started to find the peace and the healing that I needed so much.

Finding A New Direction

In the first few months of Michelle's life, I continued to follow Alan's advice and tried to read a little from my Bible each day. In all honesty the words meant little to me but I tried to take on board those verses which spoke of God's faithfulness.

Michelle and I having fun

It was during that time that the verse from Isaiah 40:11, which had been so special to me in London, came back to me. "He tends his flock like a shepherd: He gathers the lambs in his arms and carries them close to his heart; He gently leads those that have young." Now, those last words too were to hold a special place in my heart.

I also felt that it was important to try and go out each day although I had no particular place to go, but as time rolled on I knew that it gave purpose to my day and Michelle enjoyed it too.

The fact that I had acknowledged my feelings actually made them easier to deal with within myself but I still felt really condemned and told no-one of the difficulties I had.

Alan continued to write and encourage me on a regular basis and for that I was deeply grateful. I am sure that it was that encouragement that enabled me to take the step of going to both the Mums and Toddlers and the Young Wives groups that were held at the church.

The second week that I was at the Young Wives group, an announcement was made that there would be an opportunity, the following week, for individual prayer. I was absolutely sure that that was what I needed.

In the days that followed I felt positively sick at the prospect of being prayed for and when the day arrived could barely face my breakfast. Undaunted, the time arrived and at last I allowed those around me to pray for me and lay hands on me.

Such peace filled my heart and it was as if all the burdens of the past couple of years were just lifted from me. I no longer felt angry at people's ignorance and I felt a new direction in my life. I knew that that didn't mean that everything would automatically be right overnight but it did mean that I had made a start.

Although Mitch had not known what was to happen that morning, he knew as soon as I came home that something had happened to me and I hoped that he wouldn't soon be disappointed.

As the days went by, the new peace in my heart meant so much. It wasn't all easy and I still had so much to learn but I did have that certainty that God was with me every step of the way.

I found myself experiencing several problems after the pregnancy. The change of hormones in my body, which had during pregnancy caused the appliance to stick like superglue, now had the reverse effect.

The appliance would literally, with no warning, leak and come away from the skin very fast. It could be really devastating and on occasions would happen several times within a day and regularly at night. Nightfeeds were interspersed with changing the appliance and it was no wonder that at times I wandered round like a zombie.

I had also experienced problems with the stoma retracting faster than my stomach. This had been overcome by using a special convex insert (supplied by ConvaTec), pushing the stoma back out. Relief was instant and I was just so grateful. I continued to use the insert for some while and it was a real lifeline.

The final problem was not to be so easily overcome. I would get a sensation that felt as if there was a blockage or a kink in the system, causing intense pain. Eventually it would right itself and the urine would start to flow again but it was no joke. As time went on, it became apparent that a blockage of some sort had probably been caused by the pregnancy and it was obvious that something would have to be done about it.

It was two years before surgery was undertaken and an experience which left many memories. My mother had kindly undertaken to stay with Mitch and Michelle and I knew they were in good hands. The hospital was quite run down and the staffing levels extremely low. The staff themselves worked really hard and couldn't have been kinder.

I was in a ward of eight beds and it soon became apparent that there was one main feature of any conversation. Either you were someone who could "go" or you were someone who couldn't! There didn't seem to be any in-betweens and whichever one you were, how much you could do was strictly measured. I was a good twenty or thirty years younger than anyone else on the ward and felt very out of place.

On the morning of the operation, I was trying very hard to keep my mind on other things when the lady next door started up. "Ah well," she said, "the operating table is much like the butcher's block. They just chop you about a bit and then roll you back together again."

I pushed my mouth shut with my hand and made up my mind that that wasn't really true. As I looked round the rest of the ward and realised that all eyes were upon me, I began to think that perhaps they weren't too sure either.

A few minutes later the trolley arrived to take me to theatre and the hard pressed staff realised that I was neither gowned nor pre-med'ed. Throwing on the usual tie-less gown that covered nothing, I vaulted onto the trolley and thought, "Well, this is a new way of going about it."

Jabbing a needle in my backside, they wheeled me off to theatre. I really wondered why they bothered with the pre-med, it didn't have time to work before I was being given the real thing.

The pain when I awoke was something I had not been prepared for and it was some while before I got out of bed and stood upright. When I did, it soon became apparent that all was not well. The world was a very giddy place.

I was investigated and it transpired that my neck had been overstretched in some way under the anaesthetic. I returned home encased in a collar. For those who knew I had gone in for some kind of abdominal surgery, their bemused faces said it all!

It was during Michelle's early months that I had discovered another invaluable service. A distributor of stoma care products (Life Delta Ltd (Healthlink)) was now able to deliver all my prescription needs direct to my home at no cost to me. Not only was the service invaluable, but the friendships made and professional advice available were a real boon.

As I had begun to find my feet again in the real world, I knew there was one other issue that I had found hard. Whilst I loved being a mother and had really come to appreciate all the joys of motherhood, my mind was one that had always been stimulated by work and I genuinely missed that challenge.

A new and unexpected challenge soon arrived in my life. As a consequence of the pregnancy, I had made contact with other people with urostomies and I had been approached to take on the job of secretary for the local branch of the Urostomy Association.

With very little idea of what it was all about, I agreed to take it on. I soon found that the job of secretary was one that was both hard work and yet very rewarding.

The Urostomy Association had been set up in 1971 by a group of people who realised the special needs of people with a urostomy. The aim had been to provide information and help in whatever way possible, to those who were about to, or had already, undergone surgery of this kind. Their aim was to help those people to resume as full a life as possible with real confidence.

Over the years that followed, together with the help of a faithful committee, we tried to make the meetings as informal as possible. We wanted to have both the opportunity to socialise and also to be of practical help in every way possible.

I made so many wonderful friends and yet again I felt privileged to have friends like that. I always came home from the meetings challenged and inspired by the needs and the people I met.

The meetings were only a part of the work that was done. Spreading the word that the Association was available was a huge task. Still, it seemed that incontinence or anything linked to it, was taboo.

After all, many of the people who underwent surgery did so as a result of cancer and yet still "the bag" was something you didn't talk about. It could be something that any one of us might face any day and in this age of plain speaking I was saddened by the public response.

There were so many ways that we could help and encourage. It started by being available to anyone facing surgery who might like to chat with someone who already had a stoma. Time and again, people would be so encouraged to meet somebody who had already undergone surgery but who looked no different from anyone else on the street.

Once surgery had been undertaken, the next help that might be needed was to find the best possible appliances and any other supplies that might be helpful.

There were the practical needs of helping people to do all the things that they had done before. Swimmers needed to know of swimming costumes that were available with the special needs of the ostomate in mind.

For those wanting to travel, there was much practical help and advice available. There were also leaflets written in different languages for those who might face problems with customs.

If it was pregnancy, then there too there was practical advice and information about problems that could occur and how best to cope with them. It didn't matter what the problem was, every effort was made to meet the need.

In the seven years that I undertook the job of secretary, many times the job was really hard but it was always worthwhile.

As I looked back over the two years since Michelle's birth, there was no doubting that the healing of the post-natal depression had been through prayer and the laying on of hands. Nonetheless, so many other things had helped in the days that followed but when all was said and done, the road ahead had still been one of learning.

I still had to live with the same problems of misunderstanding of the disabled. I still had to deal with many gruelling physical demands upon me and had I known what lay ahead, I am sure I would have shrunk from it.

On The Move

Although we loved our little flat and all that it had meant to us, as Michelle grew into a lovely little girl, we were aware of its limitations. The garden was tiny and unfenced and the front door very close to a busy road. We had thought hard about what we should do and started searching the market for a bungalow that we might be able to buy.

As the endless trek began around the estate agents, we were soon aware that our options were limited. Not only were we limited by finance but, because of that, many of the bungalows were small and very inappropriate for Mitch's needs.

So it was that one morning, with little optimism, I had set out to view another property. At first glance, it was very obvious that the estate agent needed a new pair of glasses!

The so called "decorative wall and patio" were far from sightly. I could have pushed the wall over myself and the garden had not been touched in years. The "two apple trees" was one very puny affair that divided halfway up the trunk. Internally there was little improvement but somewhere in my mind's eye, I could see the potential that lay there.

Further visits followed and Mitch's heart must have sunk before he ever reached the front door step. The drive was a mess, there was a large step and threshold at the front door and he must have thought I'd lost a screw.

The work involved in making this our new home was going to be nothing short of horrendous but somehow it felt like God's place for us. When our offer was accepted and the details fell into line, we had to trust that God would see us through.

There were certain alterations that had to be made before we could move in. The bathroom and toilet, which lay alongside each other with separate entrances, had to be turned into one room. The bath and sink needed replacing both through old age and suitability for Mitch. We also felt that, if at all possible, replacement windows should be installed throughout before our arrival.

As the bungalow had been empty for some while, as soon as contracts were exchanged, work began. The builders came in and set to work on the bathroom and toilet and soon we began to see signs of the new layout.

Completion came and went and the bathroom was well underway. Just two days before we were due to move in, the new windows were to be fitted. Delivery of the windows had been a few days earlier and it had taken some time to persuade the delivery men that the windows were not to be left in the garden but inside the living room. On the morning of the day the windows were to be fitted, I set off very early to let the workman in.

As I left the tranquillity of our old flat, I began to notice the signs that all was not well. Although we had been aware that it had been a stormy night, nothing could have prepared me for the sight that lay all around.

Trees lay across the road, fences and walls were flattened, buildings were damaged and an air of stunned silence filled the atmosphere. As I pulled up at the drive of our new bungalow, I could have cried.

Sitting in the car, staring at the sight before me, I hardly dared to go and investigate further. The fences were all down and one had even smashed right through our next door neighbours' front door. The roof of the bungalow was littered with holes and the rain was pouring through.

I braced myself to investigate inside and tentatively searched the building. The rain was pouring through the kitchen ceiling and I really didn't know where to start. If there was one consolation, it was only that the new windows were safe and but for an argument with the delivery men, they would have been in pieces in the garden.

The days that followed were like a nightmare. Not only was all the packing to be finished but I spent hours crawling on my stomach amongst the joists of the roof. The rain was pouring in throughout the loft and I had used every conceivable item to try to contain it.

Rushing round the local do-it-yourself shop, I had grabbed some of the last tarpaulins on the shelf and grovelling on my belly in the loft, eased them to the furthest corner of the eaves. I had bruises in places I didn't know it was possible to have bruises.

I could not have been more relieved than when, two days later, Dad arrived with a trailer full of tiles for the roof and fencing panels for the garden. He put his hand to skills he had never previously had to use and, before many more days were up, the roof was watertight once more.

The first months in our new home were really tough, tempers were frayed and there were many times when we wondered what on earth we had done. There was no heating whatsoever in the bungalow and it was really cold.

The central heating was due to be fitted and several weeks in succession the company phoned with some garbled excuse as to why it couldn't be done. Alf, who had been so good to us in the past, set sail on the kitchen. The whole kitchen had to be gutted and started again from scratch.

Social Services agreed to make up a temporary ramp to the front door, but despite that, Mitch had on one occasion tipped himself over backwards, cracking the back of his head on the concrete floor. I can still hear the thud as he crashed over backwards and as I ran to help him, I really wondered what I would find.

Although the bathroom had been done in the main by the builders, all the making good, the tiling and flooring was still to be done. The drive eventually had to be ramped and a new wider front door fitted. A patio and ramp had to be created at the back of the building and it was months before we could begin to see a light at the end of the tunnel.

Our rapport with the builders had been far from good. Many errors had been made and the patio had had to be destroyed and remade due to poor workmanship.

I must have made countless trips to the tip, so much so that the men in charge began to view me with great suspicion. It became evident that they doubted it was household waste and that perhaps I was dumping business waste which was not allowed.

I took backbreaking loads of tiles, old cupboards and units, enormous loads of rubbish that had been left in the loft and bags and bags of garden waste. It was not only the physical demands but the meticulous details needed to make every part of the bungalow as accessible and functional as possible from Mitch's point of view.

I will never know how we survived those months. Emotions ran high and it can only have been God's keeping that took us through. As before, our family and faithful friends had walked the extra mile to see us through and I think they were as proud as we were when the bungalow at last began to feel like our home.

It was just as we were beginning to revel in seeing the finishing touches that I found that I was pregnant. It shouldn't have been possible but all the outward signs and the nausea told me it was true.

For a few days we felt stunned but when the confirmation came from the health centre that the test was positive, a little pang of excitement bubbled up in my heart. It was, in fact, what I would have wanted but we had always felt that one miracle was enough, we couldn't expect another.

After all, the statistics showed that the risk of having a spina bifida child rose dramatically in the second pregnancy. But now the fact remained that I was pregnant and we had to believe that God was in control.

As the days passed, such excitement filled my heart. I really wanted that baby and felt that this was God's confirmation that the pregnancy was right. In my mind I began to settle in to the enjoyment of the pregnancy but all too soon my happiness was shattered.

My father was staying and our faithful friend, Alf, and he, were insulating and boarding the loft. The bedroom was filled with the contents of the loft but as it became apparent that all was not well, I was sent to bed to rest.

In due course the doctor came out to see me and I really wondered what he thought as he made his way round the piles of debris in the room. It wasn't our own G.P. and I was so wound up with the thought of losing the baby that when he said, "Show us your tummy," I did just that.

"What on earth is that?" he muttered staring at the urostomy. It had never crossed my mind to say anything about the urostomy and I had certainly caught him on the hop!

There was nothing really that the doctor could say, except to take it easy and see what the next few days held. But as the days rolled on, although I still felt pregnant, I had this sense of foreboding. It was nearly two weeks before I finally went for a scan and the doctor told me, "I am sorry, Mrs Keays, you have lost the baby."

Such devastation hit me, I just didn't want to believe it. I couldn't understand why one minute God should give me what I longed for, but hadn't asked for, and then, just weeks later take it all away. Nothing made sense and I was desolate.

The Grief Of Miscarriage

If I didn't understand the reason for all that had happened, I did know that God cared. Absolutely filled up with the sadness of the news that day, that I had lost the baby, a telephone call interrupted our evening meal.

Weeks earlier I had entered a photographic competition run by the Urostomy Association. It was entitled "Quality of Life" and asked for photographs of what you considered added most to your quality of life.

I had sent a photo that I had taken of Michelle sitting "reading" the newspaper. She was only 19 months old at the time and her serious pose in the style of the true British businessman was really special.

Marjorie had phoned to tell me that this photo had won first prize. It seemed pretty ironic that, on the very day that I knew I had lost the baby I was carrying, I should have been told that this photograph, of the child that I did have, had won first prize for what added most to my quality of life. She certainly did and I was proud of her.

When the initial shock was over, I mentally and physically threw myself back into the task of completing our home. I tried to console myself with the fact that at least now I was still capable of getting on with many of the heavy tasks, but it did little to assuage the grief that I felt.

It seemed that all around me there were mums who were pregnant and I was very aware of people's reactions to me. Instead of letting me share their new babies, they were frightened to do so for fear of upsetting me.

Never was I more grateful than when a young mum came to see me and, without a moment's hesitation, dropped her new babe into my arms and said, "Here, have a cuddle!" At last I felt acceptable again.

There was another side to my sadness. Even during the first pregnancy, there had been looks and comments of dismay that Mitch and I should contemplate parenthood but now they were ones of, "...and a good thing too!" That attitude bore into my sadness more than ever I could say and was something I found very hard to deal with.

As the months rolled by and after long discussion, Mitch and I decided to try for another baby. In my mind I felt that through the miscarriage God had brought us to consider something that we had never dared to do before. Whilst I didn't understand the reason for the miscarriage, I did believe that it was God's will that we should try again.

But it wasn't to be something that happened straight away because God had other things that I needed to learn before that could happen.

After the miscarriage, I had coming up fighting. I was angry at people for the way they continued to treat us, I was angry at God because I didn't understand why the miscarriage should have happened and, as so often happens when the mind broods, I found plenty more to get angry about as well.

Although it was something I couldn't acknowledge for some while, the truth of the matter was, that deep down I knew that God needed to be all in all, if I was really to find happiness and peace that was not dependent on circumstances.

The independence that I had sought so fiercely, and to me, was the way to find fullness of life, was being sorely challenged. To give God all was like giving up my whole way of life and it really scared me. For weeks I fought a battle with God, eventually sharing those needs with the pastor and his wife.

Each day as I read my Bible, I found God challenging me to take that step and finally I knew it had to be. Phoning up the pastor of the church, I asked him if he would pray with me.

As we met together and we prayed and the pastor laid hands on me, God's peace knocked me off my feet and filled my heart. I couldn't believe that He could love ME like that. Who was I that He should wait patiently for me to invite Him to take that place in my life and then respond with such love for me?

But wherever we stand on the road of learning to give God all, there will always be more to learn. Each time I faced a difficult situation, God longed that through it, I should know more of the depth of His love for me.

Even as I had prayed that day, I knew that that wasn't the end, I had to learn to live it out in my daily life. Most of all, I think that it meant allowing God to take all the hurts and the knocks of daily life. The amazing part was, that if I allowed Him to, He did just that. If I put them in His hands, He was able take away the pain and put peace within.

If I had worked hard before the miscarriage, now I threw myself into a new dimension and, as if to cap it all, the second hurricane of the century hit the British Isles. Sitting in our home that day, Mitch and I were glad that Michelle was at school. The noise of the tiles ripping off the roof and crashing down onto the patio was quite terrifying. We really didn't know where was the safest place to be.

Yet again the fences were down and the mopping up began. I was a dab-hand at crawling face down across the joists by now but the novelty had long since worn off. Yet again it was a daily task to make my way across the joists emptying out the various containers and mopping up as I went. I was just so grateful when at last a builder came and completed the roof once more.

Setting sail on the decorating, I completed both the bedrooms and the hall. With Alf's help again, we demolished the shed and I set off once more for the tip. Dad returned and between us we laid a ton of turf in the back garden.

The builder returned and rebuilt a very tatty small extension at the back of the bungalow. When he had finished, it was my turn to render and tile the walls, paint the pipes and lay the flooring.

As if all that was not enough, I decided to attend a Business Enterprise Course with the possibility of working at home in typing, accounts and all that I had been trained to do.

In between times, I had also determined that it was time I made some new dresses for Michelle. All I can think was that I had gone into overdrive to compensate for my loss. The grief still hurt so very much but, rather than acknowledge it, I had buried it.

It was a ridiculous way to carry on and I suppose it was inevitable that I was going to have to pay the price. Just over a year after I had lost the baby, my body told me that something was wrong.

Staying away at a friend's house, I began to feel as if the floor was moving. At first I took no notice but by the time we returned home it was like living life on the ocean wave.

The next day I took myself to the doctor expecting him to tell me that I had an ear infection or something of that kind affecting my balance. What he in fact told me, totally shattered me. I was suffering from anxiety and depression.

I didn't feel as though I was suffering from anxiety and depression. The only effects I could feel were physical ones but the doctor explained to me that there were often physical symptoms and that, as I received treatment, the physical effects would lessen and the sadness and the emotional effects would be felt.

I could do little but take his word for it and his confirmation that the medication was non-addictive and returned home bewildered and concerned.

The doctor had asked me to return a week later to check that the level of medication was correct but in fact I was feeling considerably worse. The medication was increased and when I returned the following week the physical effects were greatly reduced.

It took a month for the physical effects to take their full course but in its place I had been hit by this unbelievable sadness and tearfulness. I couldn't remember ever crying so deeply and so brokenly. The day it first hit me was during a Sunday evening service and before I left the church, the pastor and his wife had promised that they would pray with me on a regular basis and I knew that I could count on them to do just that.

Depression - For Good Or For Evil

The months that followed were ones of great challenge. Whilst God had already taught me that I needed to allow Him to take the hurts in life, I now felt God taking me one step further. Instead of withdrawing from people and trying to avoid any further hurt, He actually wanted me to reach out and be involved with people.

I had often said that there were few people who knew the real me and that was absolutely true. Most of the time I hid away the real me and gave them the conformist, the person who agreed with everyone just to keep the peace and avoid being hurt.

But that action didn't give real peace, it was a self-protection scheme and a way that, on many occasions, did not honour God or help others to know Him.

To do what God wanted and really reach out in love to all people was something that was going to be totally life changing. There were obviously going to be hurts and rejections as a consequence but if I was giving them to God, I could trust Him to take me through them.

The amazing part was that, as I found this new depth of relationship with God, I actually realised that I could say with honesty that that relationship was more important than anything else.

Even the deep longing to have another child was something that I could handle with peace of mind. God knew my longing and if it was His will, as I believed it was, He would answer my prayers for a child in His own perfect timing.

Within three or four months I was able to give up the medication and I knew that that depression which I had despised so often in other people had taught me so much. It had taken away all my defences and my own self-sufficiency which stood as an enormous hurdle between me and God.

Now I knew that real life lay in a deep and meaningful relationship with God and when others failed, He never would.

Never again would I allow myself to look down on people who suffered from depression. I now knew that depression was no respecter of persons and any one of us could find ourselves in that situation.

I had also learnt that it had a physical side to it as well as a psychological one and it needed treatment in the same way as any other illness. It wasn't a case of "pulling oneself together" and as my own doctor had told me, left untreated, depression could take two to four years to heal.

It was just three or four months later that I realised I was pregnant again. My joy knew no bounds but it was also tinged with concern that another miscarriage could occur.

As each month passed, I began to be able to enjoy the pregnancy more and more. A great well of love bubbled up within me for the child that I was carrying. The pregnancy itself was very similar to the first one and the problems more quickly overcome.

Right up until days before the birth, I was deeply involved as the administrator for a Christmas Cracker project being run in the church. I had been booked for a planned Caesarean section on this occasion but, as the last days went slowly by, the pressure on the stoma was agonising. Sometimes I would lie on the bed on my side, trying to encourage the baby away from the stoma, but eventually I could take no more.

For two days in hospital the doctors put off the inevitable early Caesarean and I was just so thankful when the nurse came and told me, "You're booked for a Caesarean this afternoon. The waiting is over." My father had been staying for a few days and he and Mitch came to see me off to theatre.

The preparations seemed endless, did I have any false teeth, any false legs, anything else false? "Now don't worry if when you come round, you have a catheter," said the nurse.

"I don't think you'll find that's possible!" I told her.

"Ooh, good thing you reminded me!" she quipped.

At last I was on my way and I mentally steeled myself for the moment that I remembered so well from before. Not wanting to give the anaesthetic until the last possible moment for the sake of the baby, I found myself again surrounded by a host of gowned, masked and prepared nurses and doctors.

They almost had scalpel in hand before they finally gave the necessary injection. I was shaking like a leaf and felt like screaming, "For goodness sake, bash me on the head or something!"

As I fought to look around the room as I regained consciousness, a nurse came and put a little bundle in my arms. "You have a son, my dear, have a cuddle!" And there he lay, that second miracle of life. I felt so privileged.

The next few days were incredibly painful. The drip in my arm which supplied the pain killer was causing all sorts of problems despite having been inserted more than once. The stoma had again retracted faster than the stomach and my sense of humour was wearing rather thin. I couldn't lie down to sleep for more than a short time because the stoma seemed to retract all the more.

Both arms were by this time bandaged as a consequence of the drip, having first been plastered in a tar-like substance which oozed everywhere. Four days on, lying awake in the early hours, the tears started to roll. Just at that moment a new mother who had been brought onto the ward following the birth of her child during the night, got up slowly to make her way to the bathroom.

"Don't ANYONE crack a good joke or I'll thump 'em," she announced. "What the heck have they sewn in here . . . a brick?" she queried, hardly daring to put one foot in front of the other. As the morning progressed her comments continued and before long I was helpless with laughter, holding desperately onto my stomach. Laughing after a Caesarean was strictly disallowed.

Her sense of humour lifted my spirits once again and later that morning I was visited by the stoma care nurse. I knew them all well through the work of the Urostomy Association and soon we were working on something to help push the stoma back out. In the confines of a maternity ward with just curtains around my bed, the conversation to those within range must have really baffled.

Not long after the stoma care nurse had left, a whole bevy of doctors appeared on the scene. I guess I was a novelty and before long there were about five or six doctors and nurses behind the curtain around my bed, eager to have a look.

As the curtains were drawn back, the comments started up again, "Huh, what have you got that I haven't? How come you get all the handsome ones? The electrician came up a minute ago, I nearly sent him in an' all!"

Returning home a few days later with our new son, I could still hardly believe the great gift that God had given us. I was well aware that statistics said that I had a one-in-twenty five chance of having a spina bifida child in the first pregnancy and that statistic rose dramatically in the second. The fact that we had a son was also overwhelming. Girls featured throughout my side of the family and I had never dared to hope that I might have the gift of a daughter *and* a son.

Jonathan's early months were not easy ones. He was a very gripey baby and days and nights were both hardgoing. He was always sick after every feed and the blotchy patches, on the carpet and down my back, spoke volumes.

At four months I made up my mind that whatever anyone said about three month colic, I was adamant that there was more to it than met the eye. Speaking to the Health Visitor, she commented on the obviously pained appearance of my son and suggested that I cut out all dairy products. As I was feeding Jonathan myself, that meant that I had to give up all dairy products that would otherwise filter through to him in the breastmilk.

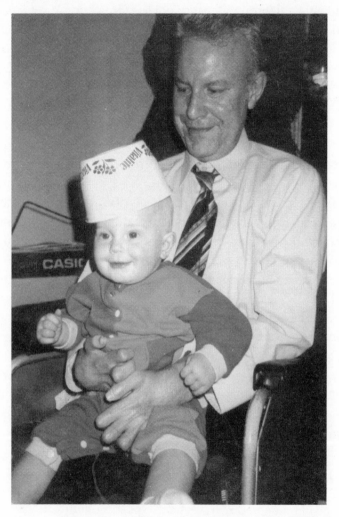

Jonathan enjoying a game with his Dad

None of us could have imagined the dramatic effect on Jonathan's well-being that was to follow. Within two days he was totally transformed. We had a son who smiled and chuckled and laughed. No more did he throw himself around in obvious discomfort. He was still sick regularly, but he was happy and so were we.

The months rolled by and our little baby grew into a toddler of very determined nature. He and Michelle had a wonderful relationship that was very special. As an older child Michelle had that ability to be able to appreciate him fully and be a "mother" to him. We counted ourselves very privileged to have two children who obviously cared so much for each other.

But as Jonathan grew into a little boy, we knew that, if that relationship was to remain special, they needed their own space and Michelle in particular, a room that wasn't going to be regularly vandalised by an inquisitive little boy.

Dreading the thought of more building work, we looked into the possibility of extending the bungalow to create another bedroom. We had spent so long making the bungalow everything we wanted it to be, especially from Mitch's point of view, and any thought of moving was quickly put aside.

Soon after Jonathan's first birthday, plans were drawn up and the builders started work in the first week of June.

Facing Serious Illness

It was during the latter part of July, when the builders were hard at work on the extension, that I started to feel really exhausted. Everything seemed to take a Herculean effort, even a cup of coffee seemed to weigh pounds.

Shakiness was a real problem and at times I behaved in quite a drunken fashion, almost falling over for no apparent reason. As the symptoms persisted, the main problem was one of continuous muscle spasm in my arms which at times became very painful. It was severe enough to keep me awake at night and became a real problem.

For the first couple of weeks life went on as normal, albeit with a great struggle. One Saturday I decided to take the children for an outing to a local butterfly farm. As we set off round the various houses, I realised that I had taken on more than I could manage. Not wishing to admit defeat and embarrassed to leave almost as soon as we had arrived, I plodded on relentlessly.

Exhaustion was absolutely overwhelming, my legs were like lead weights and my body barely functioned. Eventually I could take no more and persuaded the children that we simply had to leave.

Turning to check the exit sign for the way out, all I could see was coloured patterns. Staring at it blankly for what seemed like ages, the patterns at last turned to letters, and relieved, we set off home. That became the start of what was to be one of the most testing times of my life.

Worried in the main by the visual effects of the illness, I made an appointment with my G.P. who took a blood test and said that he felt it was quite possibly a thyroid problem.

Relieved at the prospect of medication and relief from the symptoms, I carried on with new hope. But by the time I returned to his surgery the following week for the result of the blood test, I felt even worse. I simply could not hold my arms up for more than a few seconds. Simple everyday tasks of brushing my hair, hanging out the washing or doing the washing up became acts of grit determination.

The thyroid test proved negative and the doctor set in motion a whole range of blood tests from diabetes to glandular fever. Wishing the days away, I returned a week later desperate for answers. There was nothing.

All the blood tests were normal and my doctor could only tell me that it must be a virus and I would just have to live with it until the symptoms passed. Barely outside the surgery door, the tears flowed. How was I going to live with this and carry out all the responsibilities that my family required of me?

Over a period of time, I found that the symptoms waxed and waned. Some days were those of complete and overwhelming exhaustion. My muscles burned with exhaustion. Any continuous effort to fight on just intensified the pain and sometimes the effects would last for days.

Other days I rose feeling near normal and set about the rigorous demands of life. I soon learnt that I could not just assume that all was well and pick up where I had left off. The results were inevitable.

It took three months before I really admitted to my family the full effects of the illness. Half term came and I knew that all I wanted to do was spend a week at home as quietly as was physically possible with two young children. The week was a soothing balm and the children were very patient.

For a couple of months, the physical exhaustion waned and in its place I had an almost perpetual sore throat. It wasn't until the end of December and into the new year, that the sore throat was gone and the pain and the exhaustion were back with a vengeance.

The muscle spasm by this time was everywhere. It was in my calf muscles, thighs, ankles, shoulders and arms, but worst of all, my feet. My feet were, in a sense, one of my weakest spots, affected by the spina bifida and with extremely high arches. I was learning to cope with the pain in other parts of my body but my feet were another matter.

It was about this time that I happened to read an article in a magazine. There before me, was someone describing a replica, in so many ways, of all the different symptoms that I was trying to come to terms with.

At last I knew that there was someone else out there, who knew what it was to be so exhausted, that even to brush one's hair at the start of the day, was a physical effort. It also confirmed my suspicions that I wasn't imagining the new effects that I was noticing concerning my vision, concentration and memory. All of these were starting to be affected and that in itself was quite frightening.

The symptoms that I had read about were those of the illness M.E. (Myalgic Encephalomyelitis). I had heard the name in the past and knew that it had had some bad press, not least being referred to as "Yuppie 'Flu". I also knew that there was no cure and faced the prospect with some concern.

Not saying a word to Mitch or anyone else, I wrote off for information and daily scrutinised the post for the return letter. When at last it came, I had very little doubt that M.E. was what I had.

In February half term came round again and I had rashly agreed that we would go and stay with my sister and her family in Taunton. Three days before the start of half term, things worsened considerably.

It was cold weather and I had put on a lovely thick Aran cardigan. Before breakfast was over, I had had to remove it, the weight of it on my shoulders was just too much to bear.

The day before we were due to leave, the exhaustion was the worst I had ever experienced. I felt close to collapse and just didn't know how to keep going. But as had so often happened, the next day I felt completely different. I felt very weak and lacking in strength but the exhaustion had lifted.

We managed the trip away and although tired, the change had done me good.

It was during our brief stay away that I had spent one evening having a heart to heart with my sister. I had still not said anything to anyone about the possibility of M.E. and had determined that I would not do so until someone else raised the possibility with me.

It was during this heart to heart, that my sister, as an occupational therapist, said how many of my symptoms matched those that she had seen in her patients with M.E.

Returning home after the break I returned to the doctor desperate to lay on the line just how ill I felt. My own G.P. was on holiday and I wondered how much I could convey to someone who knew very little of me. But I was to return encouraged. I was to be referred to a consultant physician at the local hospital.

Although the doctor had not used the word "M.E.", he had said that he felt it was a post viral condition of some kind. With both the comments of the doctor and my sister, I felt that it was time to tell one or two of our closest friends and a few others, what had been suggested.

I was already aware, that as I had no option but to fulfil my responsibilities for the family, my illness was an invisible one. Though it might take everything I had to get through the day, if I made any comments about how I felt, it was met with blank unbelief. Very soon I felt really humiliated and vowed not to speak about it.

I received nothing but complete support from my family and closest friends but the hurt induced by those who did not understand was at times harder to bear than the illness itself.

The decision not to speak out about the illness was, in hindsight, a bad one. It alienated me from those around me and effectively hid the problems away.

The progression of the illness was now taking on a new and at times really devastating effect. The muscles in my eyes were being affected and I was finding it extremely difficult to concentrate.

I had written in my diary that it was as if I could see everything, but that there was a delayed response of understanding and interpreting. My memory too, was very much affected and I would meet with people whom I had known for years and their names were totally eradicated from my mind.

Occasionally I would find myself reversing words and generally tripping over my speech. At first these effects seemed quite slight but rapidly the vision and concentration deteriorated until at times it was almost impossible to read or even watch the television. The effort of concentration was so extreme that it was impossible to carry on.

As time went on, the reality of the things that I was finding difficult came home to me. It was now impossible to read a book in bed. There was simply no way that I could lie down and hold a book to read. The pain that it caused in my arms was unbearable and, inevitably, in due course the book ended up on the floor.

The music that I enjoyed also became a thing which regularly defeated me. I simply could not interpret the music fast enough and if I did manage it, the effort of doing so rapidly stopped all enjoyment.

It seemed that the simple pleasures of life were rapidly diminishing and I could not come to terms with how devastating the illness had become. And yet to all intents and purposes, to everyone else, I was no different.

The wait for the appointment at the hospital seemed endless but finally, two months later, the day arrived. The examination was very thorough and blood tests were taken. In his opinion, the diagnosis was one of Post Viral Fatigue

Syndrome, subject to nothing else showing up on the tests that he had sent away.

It was another three months before that letter of confirmation came that nothing else had been found and Post Viral Fatigue Syndrome was his official diagnosis. Whilst that diagnosis did not change the fact that there were no easy answers, it did in some way help to know that it was official in the eyes of the medical team.

In the intervening months my condition had deteriorated considerably. The visual effects had become extreme and the exhaustion all consuming. I had been trying to cope with potty-training Jonathan and there were times when I simply lay down on the floor as he sat on his potty beside me.

Peeling potatoes at the sink regularly defied me and at times the effort required to use a knife and fork and eat a meal was almost beyond me. And yet, thankfully, there were times of relief.

My parents became aware of the struggle going on and generously gave of their time on several occasions to stay and help out. I don't know what would have happened if I had not had that help. Not only physically but mentally their help was a lifeline.

Through all the eleven months that the illness had been with me, I had struggled to continue to provide everything that my family needed. As far as I was able, I was determined to get the children to all the things that they wanted to do. Why should they suffer, particularly as it seemed that it was not going to be a short-term thing?

When at last each day was over, I would fall into a chair and could cope with nothing more. I was fiercely independent and did not want to have to ask for help. Giving was easy, receiving was not. Perhaps in a sense, I felt that having to ask for, and receiving help, was admitting to failure. It wasn't true, but it takes a very special person to be able to get alongside and come into the home of a fiercely independent person, do their work for them and not make them feel inadequate.

So the battle rolled on week after week, month after month. I was not going to admit defeat and yet I was crying out for help. When my mother suggested that I should actually go right away for a few days holiday to a Centre of Christian Healing, a little ray of hope lit up in my heart. I longed for that time aside and for time alone with God.

God's Comfort

When at last I set off for the Harnhill Centre of Christian Healing, although I knew I needed so much the respite and refreshing of those days apart, I felt as if I was abandoning the family.

It wasn't true, of course, as my parents once more had taken up the reins of caring for the family and I had no worries, knowing that they were more than adequately catered for.

Arriving amidst the tranquillity of the Cotswold landscape, I knew that these days had been planned by God but never more so than the following morning.

As a resident for the week, we were given the opportunity to take part in a "Quiet Day" that was being held at the Centre. The theme for the morning came from the passage in Luke 10 referring to the story of Mary and Martha. Martha was running around undertaking all the household chores while Mary sat at Jesus' feet. "Today," we were told, "You have earned the right to stop and be still."

She continued by saying that there was a time to be a Martha and a time to be a Mary. Today we were to be a Mary. I could have cried. Relief flooded in. Here was God's specific word that today I had earned the right to sit at His feet and spend time with Him.

Throughout the day, we continued to look at different passages where Mary and Martha had met with Jesus. Some very special thoughts were drawn out of those passages. Mary had met with Jesus in a time of great pain and Jesus had wept with her. What a wonderful thought that He had shared so personally in her pain and no doubt did that for me too.

I was sure that God had much to teach me that week. I knew that there weren't going to be any easy answers but that God had some very special treasures to share with me in a time of darkness. God had never said that the Christian life was going to be an easy one and I felt now, more than ever, that He was going to use these dark and difficult times to teach me things that I would never have learnt when life was easy.

It was a very special week which meant so much and if there was one overall theme for me, it was that I had to continue to trust God whatever my circumstances.

I arrived home at teatime on the Friday afternoon with a new sense of purpose. The family were pleased to see me and the children had so much to tell me. Friends phoned to found out how I was and it took a couple of days before I had really been able to share with Mitch much of what had happened. But even before I had, Mitch knew that there was a change in me and saw the happiness and sense of peace within.

It was at church the following weekend that I was approached by one of the leaders, who had only just heard about my illness. Immediately he asked if the church could pray for me that morning and anoint me with oil.

As they prayed for me at the front of the church and anointed me with oil, I realised that that act was almost a sacrifice on my part. I was at the front of the church expressing my need of their fellowship and prayers and ultimately their support in the days ahead.

The following months were to be a training ground for so many changes in the way I lived my daily life. Never before, as an adult, had I faced serious illness. As a child, I had been too young to consider the implications of the spina bifida. By the time I had been old enough to do so, many of the major problems had been overcome. But the M.E. was something different and the future very unknown. As a wife and mother with responsibilities and commitments to fulfil, and fears for my future, I was genuinely concerned and confused.

All my life I had wanted to live "life in all its fullness." The circumstances of my birth, and the determination that had been rooted within me, that no exceptions were to be made for me, had made me intensely independent. It was that independence that was now being challenged in the most forceful way.

My independence said I could do anything if I worked hard enough. It said that help from others was a sign of failure. When my independence was challenged again by people's attitude to disabled people, I was doubly tormented. I felt that I had done everything within my power to prove myself in my early life and again in our life as a "disabled" family and yet people belittled us and made us out to be "a penny short of a pound."

As the days and weeks slipped by, I began to realise the enormity of God's love for each one of us. As I looked at Jesus' own experiences in life, it was abundantly obvious that He had been through every conceivable kind of suffering and could identify intensely with our own daily lives.

There were times when I felt so alone. M.E. was not something which everyone knew about although more publicity was coming through in the media. However what publicity did prevail was not always helpful and there seemed so much misunderstanding.

As I read the passage of Jesus in Gethsamene, knowing that He faced death on the cross, and going aside to pray in deep anguish over all that He knew lay ahead, the disciples had on each occasion fallen asleep oblivious to His distress. Who was I to say that God didn't enter 100 percent into my problems? He had suffered loneliness beyond anything I would ever know, and His heart welled up with understanding for me as it did for all the suffering people of the world.

I had found too that, as I was more open about the illness, people refused to believe that the effects were caused by M.E. The comments that hurt the most were from those who said I was suffering from depression. I had been there before and I knew without any shadow of a doubt that this was not depression.

I was not in any way suffering from the loss of motivation that is classic in depression. Quite the reverse, I really wanted to get up and go. My frustration was in the inability of my body to physically do that and if I was ever emotional or tearful, it was that very frustration that caused it.

And so again God's Word came home to me. Psalm 31:20 said: " . . . in your dwelling you keep them safe from the strife of tongues." It was down to me to seek refuge in God's loving arms.

I had to acknowledge too that Jesus knew what it was to suffer pain. He must have suffered on the cross the worst pain that one could ever dare to entertain. I had read in a passage by Selwyn Hughes that described Jesus' physical pain in this way:

"The cut, crushed nerves would scream out in fierce agony, while the body temperature would mount until dizziness and disorientation set in. Every movement of the body, however slight, would have added to the intense physical torture, tearing the wounds and making them larger and wider. Normally death came by asphyxiation."

Jesus was more than able to identify in every way with both the physical and mental disorientation that I had and was continuing to experience.

And finally I realised too that when at times I had felt humiliated, belittled and scorned, I had someone in Jesus who had suffered the ultimate scorn and shame. He had been stripped of his clothes, whipped, spat on, beaten, derided and finally slung on a cross before the eyes of a mocking crowd and still He had loved them.

In Jesus I had someone who could identify with each situation I faced and He longed to be there sharing the pain and helping me through it.

But it wasn't just the negative that God answered so graciously. Just before I had gone to stay at Harnhill, the overwhelming exhaustion and extreme pain had made me realise that I had no option but to ask for help from Social Services. It had taken a couple of months for the details to be organised but their response had been so positive.

Despite the fact that services were stretched beyond the limits, they had provided me with both help with the children and in the home and I was so grateful. I found it extremely hard to allow them to do my work while I was expected to set that time aside for rest, but I knew it had to be.

It was the first time that the Home Care lady had visited. In the course of conversation, she mentioned that she was in fact retired and only working part-time. Her words hit home like a bullet. How could I, as a young person, sit there and allow a retired lady to do my housework? I almost shouted with frustration, "Well, that does it, Lord! That takes the biscuit!"

But God in His mercy let me see that even He had so often been dependent on other people. He had been born in someone else's stable, generously welcomed into other people's homes, supported out of other people's means, received food from the hands of a young boy, rode into Jerusalem on another man's donkey, had had the cross on which He was crucified carried by another man and finally was buried in someone else's tomb.

Whilst I found it very easy to be a giver, I had to learn to receive as well. It was not an act to be despised but one that I needed to accept and appreciate for its generosity. Why should I not allow someone else the pleasure that I received from giving?

So it was, that over the ensuing months I learnt to accept with a gracious heart not only the help of family but the food cooked by a lovely widow from the church, the provision of easily prepared food by another much loved friend, the mowing of my lawns by a neighbour and the care and concern of so many others. I had a lot to learn.

Indeed as the passage in Psalm 84:6 said: "As they pass through the Valley of Baca (Weeping), they make it a place of springs." This time of testing could, if I allowed it, be a place of good and new things.

Progress - A Step At A Time

As the months passed by I began to progress in my recovery mainly, I felt, for two reasons. Firstly, the help that I had received through Social Services had taken from me the jobs that I found hardest and which caused most exhaustion and muscle pain. I was so grateful for all that they did and really appreciated the friendships that we made through them.

Secondly, I had also heard of and read about a diet that many M.E. patients had found beneficial. It was based on the problem of candida and whilst I was not a medical person and had no proof of its validity, some of what I read made me think very seriously about it.

Candida is caused by the loss of essential bacteria in the body reducing the ability to fight infection. These essential bacteria can be killed by prolonged use of antibiotics and I was well aware that I had been on a low dose of antibiotics throughout both pregnancies and through urinary and other infections.

I also noted reference to the fact that both Athlete's Foot and mouth ulcers were linked with this problem, both of which had recently become a problem.

I decided that there was no harm in giving the diet a try and at that stage my understanding was that refined sugar was the main cause of aggravating the problem and decided to cut it out.

It was the summer holidays by this time and for about a month I was absolutely rigid in my avoidance of sugar and slowly began to see some progress. Unfortunately towards the end of the holiday, we had several visitors and then went on an extended family holiday. With others cooking the meals, I found it difficult to maintain and let the diet slip. Within a relatively short time, I felt I had deteriorated again.

Not making any assumptions on that alone, I read more about the diet and realised that there were in fact two main items to be avoided, sugar and yeast. Other items were mentioned too and I started again in a very disciplined fashion. Within two months, the muscle pain was barely recognisable from what it had been before and I was thrilled.

Not only that, but I had lost the problems with Athlete's Foot and the mouth ulcers and I had also lost about nine pounds in weight which I had put on for no apparent reason soon after the M.E. had started. Having returned to my original weight, the loss stopped and my weight remained constant.

When Christmas came I decided that it was time for the ultimate test. Over Christmas and the ensuing month I brought back into my diet, bread and many other foods containing yeast and sugar. Slowly but surely my progress started to regress, all the old problems came back and I determined that for the foreseeable future I would have to go back and maintain the diet.

I found that as long as I maintained that diet the progress continued. That didn't mean however that the M.E. was gone. Many times I was lulled into a false sense of security believing that all was well. Time and again I found myself overstretching the mark and all the muscle pain and problems would start to return.

As the second anniversary of my illness neared, I had to acknowledge that whilst I felt a different person, the illness lingered and a relapse could so easily be triggered. Limitations were still rigidly in place and I was going to have to learn to abide by them.

Even more now, people could not understand that the M.E. remained. I was seen to be managing more so I must be better. The problem appeared to be gone. It wasn't.

If I had made progress on the physical side, sadly I had deteriorated with the visual problems and the loss of memory and lack of concentration. At times it was extreme beyond compare.

During one particularly difficult week, I had found it almost impossible to cross a road. Because my concentration was so poor and so slow, it took what seemed like ages to work out where all the cars were, and by the time I had, they had all moved and I was in danger of stepping out under a car.

The physical effects had been extremely difficult to live with but the neurological ones were even worse. Somehow pain seemed more acceptable and understandable but the neurological symptoms were both very frustrating and at times frightening.

Throughout all this time, I had been so much helped and encouraged by my daily readings of the Bible. If there was one thing that I was learning more and more, it was of the love of God for me and the fact that it never changed and was utterly dependable.

God's love wasn't based on what I did or how I felt. It wasn't earned, it wasn't achieved. God loved me in a way that was almost incomprehensible and as nobody else ever could.

Psalm 139:13-16 said, "For you created my inmost being; you knit me together in my mother's womb...My frame was not hidden from you when I was made in the secret place. When I was woven together in the depths of the earth, your eyes saw my unformed body. All the days ordained for me were written in your book before one of them came to be."

As I looked back over my life, there had been good times, hard times, sad times and happy times. There had been many battles on the way but the hardest one of all had been realising that I, in myself, was not able to conjure up "life in all its fullness." Only God was able to do that.

By virtue of my birth and medical circumstances, my parents had determined to bring me up as an independent person who was able to contribute to life and live it to the full. For their decision, I was just so grateful.

My independent streak had not been wrong but I had had to learn to channel it aright. The battles that I had had were, on almost each and every occasion, related to a wrong use and understanding of that independence.

As I concluded the final chapters of this book, I read a passage from Colin Urquhart's book, "My Dear Child..." The book was written as a series of letters from the Heavenly Father's heart to the hearts of his children.

The three sisters! Kate, Sal and Jane

The extended family meet up

One passage spoke so clearly to me. It spoke of God watching over the circumstances of his children's birth, parents and family. I was absolutely sure that God had done that for me. It went on to speak of the difficulties and traumas of growing up and there the question was posed, "Did I [God] plan these?"

God's answer was, "Well, my child, I saw you through them all, didn't I? Those difficulties were important in building your character and in teaching you to look to me and depend on my love." I knew without any doubt that I would never have learnt so many of the important truths and values in life had those challenges not been mine.

The passage ended by encouraging that, if God could see his children through past experience, he could certainly see them through the future. I had no doubt about that either - I had such a good God!

Jonathan and Michelle

Epilogue

It took approximately four years for my recovery from the M.E. to be complete. That recovery was just so special - almost like being given one's life back.

So what had I learnt over the years through all that had happened? What had I learnt about life and the values that were important?

From my youngest days, I had learnt that stoma surgery was not something to be feared, in fact, quite the reverse. For me and so many others, the surgery had given me the freedom to live a full and varied life. I could honestly say that nothing had been denied me by my surgery, in fact quite the opposite, it had turned my life around.

I had also learnt though, that whoever we are and despite our greatest efforts, there will always be times of trial and crisis in our lives. We each needed each other and we had to be able to give as well as receive. Both were equally important and were the basis of a lifestyle of love and respect for each other.

Another issue which had become very plain, was that there were some areas of life which, despite the so-called age of plain speaking, remained taboo. This book was intended to meet such a need and although, in the main, is aimed at the needs of the stoma patient, I believe it has touched on other issues such as disability and depression as well as the difficulties of coping with suffering and serious illness.

I have shared my heart in a way that will no doubt make me very vulnerable. I do so because I wish to unwrap and challenge some of the misplaced standards and values held by the society in which we live. I also wish to encourage and stand alongside those whose lives are touched by any of these issues. My Christian faith has been at the centre of all that I have learnt and therefore, that too, must be a part of the story.

In conclusion, I would like to ensure that all stoma patients are aware of the help available from the support associations (addresses follow). For every copy of the book sold, a donation will be made into a fund to be divided between the three associations.

I would also like to pay tribute to the two companies who have not only sponsored this book but who have, over the years, provided the quality equipment that has been essential in enabling me to live life to the full. Also to the distributor who has not only supported this book but delivered my prescription requirements over the years.

Most of all, I owe the greatest debt of thanks to my family and friends whose support has been quite fantastic. I would not dare to mention any names - there are just too many to mention.

<u>To:</u>
Dad, Mum, Jane and Sal,
Mitch, Michelle and Jonathan,
"I love you
and
thank you
for all that you mean to me."

Useful Addresses

The Urostomy Association
Central Office
Buckland
Beaumont Park
DANBURY
Essex
CM3 4DE
Tel. (01245) 224294

ia (The Ileostomy and Internal Pouch Support Group)
Amblehurst House
PO Box 23
MANSFIELD
Notts
NG18 4TT
Tel. (01623) 28099

The British Colostomy Association
15 Station Road
READING
Berkshire
RG1 1LG
Tel. (01189) 391537

Bibliography

Colin Urquhart, *My Dear Child...*, Hodder & Stoughton Ltd, 1990.

Grace Sheppard, *An Aspect of Fear*, Darton, Longman & Todd Ltd, 1989.